Divine Reflections

in Living Things

Eva Peck

© 2013 by Eva Peck

All rights reserved

Except for any fair dealing permitted under the Copyright Act, no part of this book may be reproduced by any means without prior permission of the author and publisher.

Photography: Alexander Peck with the exception of
Pages 24 and 69, which is courtesy of www.freedigitalphotos.net
Page 78, which was purchased from www.dreamstime.com
Page 108, which is the credit of Jindrich Degen

Graphic design and cover design: Eva Peck

Bible quotes and paraphrases taken from the HOLY BIBLE, NEW INTERNATIONAL VERSION. Copyright © 1973, 1978, 1984 by International Bible Society. Used by permission of Zondervan Publishing House. All rights reserved.

National Library of Australia Cataloguing-in-Publication entry

Author: Peck, Eva.
Title: Divine reflections in living things / Eva Peck;
        Alexander Peck, photography.

ISBN: 9780987500304 (pbk.)

Subjects: Biology--Religious aspects.
           Nature--Religious aspects.
           Spiritual formation.
           Spiritual life.

Other Authors/Contributors: Peck, Alexander.

Dewey Number: 248.2

The book can be purchased online through
www.heavens-reflections.org or www.pathway-publishing.org

Dedicated to
the Maker of all creatures great and small,
and those made in the Creator's image.

Other Books by the Same Author

Divine Reflections in Times and Seasons
Divine Reflections in Natural Phenomena
Divine Insights from Human Life

Co-author of:
Pathway to Life – Through the Holy Scriptures
Journey to the Divine Within – Through Silence, Stillness and Simplicity

Acknowledgments

First, I would like to thank the Great God for enabling, inspiring and blessing this publication.

I must also thank my husband, Alex, for his encouragement and support. He is always ready to help with editing and to give helpful advice. Without his valuable input, this book would not have come out as it has.

Contents

Preface 8

Introduction 12

Camouflage.. 15

   The Camouflaged God 16
   Perceiving the Camouflaged God 18

Birth... 24

   Prenatal Development...................................... 25
   Spiritual Parallels with Prenatal Development..... 26
   Special Births... 32
   The Firstborn... 34

Of Cats, Humans and God 37

   Insights from Desert Cats.................................. 38
   Individual Differences...................................... 40
   Loving All Kinds 42
   Virtue of Stillness and Patience 44

Pigeons 48

   Of Birds and Thoughts 50
   A New Generation of Pigeons........................... 53
   Other Analogies 57

Insights from Frogs... 61

   Frog Life Cycle 61
   Spiritual Parallels 63
   The Transformation 65

Butterfly Metamorphosis 69

    Life Cycle of a Butterfly 70
    Physical and Spiritual Parallels 72

Emperor Penguins 78

    Penguin Life Cycle 79
    Spiritual Parallels 82

The Amazing Date Palm 89

    History 90
    Growth of Palm Trees 90
    Fruit of the Palm 91
    Palms in the Bible 92
    Spiritual Parallels 93

Pond Flowers 96

    Flowers as a Life Metaphor 97

Growing Cherry Tomatoes 100

    Lessons for Life 102

About the Author 108

More About the Author's Other Books 110

Other Resources 112

Readers' Comments 114

About Pathway Publishing 117

Preface

Ever since I was a young child, nature fascinated me. All creatures big and small attracted my attention, as did trees, plants, flowers, shells, rocks, and even footprints in the dust. Spring blossoms carpeting the forest floor, buds opening into brand new leaves, colourful fluttering butterflies – all this and more was a never-ending source of wonder. Not surprisingly, I decided to study biological sciences in high school and later at university.

Even now, decades later, I am still finely attuned to the natural environment. Both the animate realm of animals, birds, reptiles, insects, and the diverse world of plants, as well as the inanimate surroundings of sky, sea and mountains speak to my heart.

While I was always in tune with nature, the Divine was not a part of my thinking as a child. On the contrary, atheistic Communist teaching more or less convinced me and my classmates from a young age that there was no God. After all, we were told, Yuri Gagarin, the first man to visit outer space and orbit the earth in 1961, didn't see God up there.

It was only in my late teens that my eyes were opened to God's existence. I then began to see behind everything in nature a Designer, Creator, Life-Giver and Sustainer. Purposeless, haphazard evolution no longer made sense as an answer to the order, harmony and complexity of the natural world. For many years, I rejected the idea of evolution altogether, believing in a six-day divine creation as described in the biblical book of Genesis.

However, as I continued to read on the subject of origins, especially books by Christian or Jewish writers who were also respected scientists and tried to reconcile the apparent contradictions between the Bible and science, I couldn't deny the massive amount of evidence for an evolutionary origin of life. There had to be another interpretation of the Genesis story. As with other situations where there are divergent viewpoints, I have come to realize that a conclusion may need to hold in tension two or more alternatives. In this case, it would be a Mind behind all things (the immanent nature of the Divine in which "we [and all that exists] live, move, and have our being" – Acts 17:28), as well as natural and evolutionary processes ultimately accomplishing a divine purpose.

Increasing familiarity with the Holy Scriptures led me to perceive in the natural world a reflection of spiritual realities. These insights became the genesis of this book which is the third of a trilogy. The other two are *Divine Reflections in Times and Seasons* and *Divine Reflections in Natural Phenomena*. All three books are available through:

http://www.heavens-reflections.org (the accompanying website for the trilogy) as well as http://www.pathway-publishing.org (featuring all of our websites and publications).

Divine Reflections in Living Things and its two companion titles encourage us to take a fresh look at what is around us – to see each living thing and every process as if for the first time. The biblical writers, too, point us to the natural world to recognize divine glories – see Psalm 19 for a striking example. If we can, even briefly, stop and ponder, life and the surrounding world will start to unveil to us beautiful divine qualities such as love, wisdom, peace and joy.

This book is based on the belief that God, or a Higher Mind, is behind all that exists. However, I do not insist on a literal interpretation of all biblical accounts, as I have come to understand that the Scriptures are not intended to be a strictly scientific or historical work. Rather, the Bible reveals, often in symbolic language, God's deeds in human history and also points to unseen spiritual realities. Poetry and metaphor may be the best or only vehicles to communicate what is inexpressible in literal language.

I understand that the Divine is neither male nor female. However, to use the pronoun "it" seems inappropriate, therefore I am opting for the grammatical gender "he".

For those who desire to learn more about the biblical teachings behind the observations, footnotes provide scriptural references for the conclusions reached.

Of course, other writers have also expressed the idea that the physical world pictures spiritual realities – each in their own unique way. These are my perceptions based on my experiences and understanding of how the spiritual is reflected in the world of living things. May you, too, gain new insights as you take another look at life around you.

Eva Peck

Introduction

Jesus asked him,
"What do you want me to do for you?"
"Lord, I want to see."
Luke 18:40-41

Please open my eyes to see wonderful things in your creation.

While we may understand God as being *transcendent* as well as having become *personal* through Jesus Christ, another aspect of the Divine may be escaping us. The Scriptures reveal that God is also *immanent* and that this aspect of Divinity is all around us – "He is not far from each one of us. 'For in him we live and move and have our being.'" (Acts 17:27-28).

It's possible for us to be like the blind men that Jesus encountered on his travels – but worse still, not even realize that we are blind or missing anything. Unknowingly, we may be oblivious to the divine realities surrounding us. Just as countless camouflaged living creatures cross our paths but totally escape our attention, there is camouflaged divinity in every nook and cranny of the created order. Living things – both plants and animals – can teach us much about life, as well as giving us insights into present and future spiritual realities.

Introduction

This book proposes, like its companion volumes *Divine Reflections in Times and Seasons* and *Divine Reflections in Natural Phenomena*, that the Divine can be glimpsed in ordinary experiences – and that indeed all of life is sacred and as such teaches us about and brings us closer to God. In other words, an immanent aspect of the Divine pervades all living things, enabling us to see traces of the transcendent reality. A consciousness of the Creator's presence in the seemingly mundane will help us recognize divine qualities reflected in the creation.

Like the blind men in the Scriptures, of and by ourselves we are often unable to see the camouflaged divinity. We may well need to have our eyes opened and the divine brought to light. Then, with a desire to see and know, by looking deeper below and beyond the surface of the seemingly mundane, we will be able to glimpse the divine presence. Something as ordinary as the household cat, birds nesting in the backyard tree, or a flower bed with butterflies hovering over it – these, as well as myriads of other things around us, will enable us to discern or spot signs of the divine mystery.

This closer and deeper looking at life will also allow us to perceive the unity and interconnection ("inter-being") of all things. Everything is interrelated and interdependent, as well as containing all else –

animals depend on plants for oxygen and sometimes for food, plants need insects for pollination and thus species preservation, and all life needs and contains energy from the sun and water from the clouds for survival.

As we become open to new possibilities of seeing and begin to interpret our experiences in fresh ways, the ordinary transforms itself into the extraordinary and the previously unnoticed becomes a source of marvel!

Camouflage

The goanna crossed my path, its colour blending with the hues of the ground. It jumped into the pond and quietly waited with only its head above water – again barely noticeable among the *Salvinia* leaves. Finally the creature swam to the tree growing in the water and climbed up. It came to rest about half a metre up the trunk where it sat motionless, once more almost inconspicuous against its background. Any passerby not aware of its presence would easily miss seeing it.

Camouflage is a familiar phenomenon in nature. For many creatures, it is their chief line of defence against predators – a vital means of survival. Insects living on the ground or among leaves, such as grasshoppers, caterpillars, and praying mantises, are brown or subdued shades of green. Birds in tropical and semitropical areas, such as lorikeets, rosellas, and other parrot species blend into their surroundings with their bright-coloured attire. Some animals change colour with seasons so as not to stand out in their environment. Hares in temperate climates, for instance, grow a white winter coat to make them inconspicuous in snow, and exchange it for a light brown one in spring to blend with the surrounding hues. And remarkably, chameleons change their colour at short notice if their environment changes. Only upon closer observation do we become aware of the presence of many living creatures.

The Camouflaged God

The Creator aspect of the Divine – the Mind and Life Force in and behind all living things – not only built camouflage into nature, but one could say that God also uses camouflage. The presence of the Divine in the world is not obvious. "In faith there is enough light for those who want to believe and enough shadows to blind those who don't" wrote Blaise Pascal.

God's existence cannot be irrevocably proven or disproven. There is room for other explanations regarding the origin and existence of the universe and life, supporting the arguments of those who wish to remain atheists. At the same time, strong evidence suggests a supernatural mind behind all things. Nonetheless, when witnessing misery and suffering caused by human inhumanity or natural forces, many ask if God can indeed exist. Some theologians have also written about God's hiddenness.

All religions agree that the true and absolute Reality and Consciousness referred to as God is beyond human comprehension and expression in any language. Anything we may describe as God is only a symbol, analogy or metaphor that we can get our minds around. God is far more, far greater, and far beyond anything we can imagine or put into words. The physical world, however, contains signs and attributes of the ultimate Reality. If we realize that everything around us points to the indescribable God beyond time and space – remembering at all times that whatever we see is not God – we can catch glimpses of the Ultimate.

Perception of anything is individual and relative. How we perceive people, events, or even our surroundings depends to a large degree on our disposition, personality, knowledge, experiences, prejudices, and even our mood of the moment. The axiom that beauty is in the eye of the beholder applies in principle also to perception of what we consider to be right or true in the human realm, as well as in the realm of God and spirituality. A cynic or pessimist, shaped by his or her experiences, tends to view life negatively – people as inherently evil, the universe as unfriendly, and God as harsh or nonexistent. By contrast, an optimist's perception of life tends to be positive and hopeful.

Perceiving the Camouflaged God

God, the Divine Reality and Source of all things, is both hidden and perceivable – not unlike the goanna silently hugging the tree trunk. Only upon a closer, careful look with an open mind and heart are God's attributes and presence perceived – be it in nature, external events and circumstances, or in one's personal life. And, just as sometimes another person is needed to show us the camouflaged goanna on the tree, we may need a spiritual guide to help us discern God's presence. For those seeking to develop a greater awareness of the Divine, the following principles may be helpful.[1]

Firstly, God's attributes may be perceived in what surrounds us. We sense the transcendent in a spectacular sunrise, a brightly coloured butterfly fluttering from one flower to another, or adorable kittens romping together in play. We are awed by a star-filled, moonlit night sky, towering snow-capped mountains, or even an ancient tree of giant proportions. Human creativity in the realms of music, art, sculpture, poetry, and writing often attests to divine inspiration.

---

[1] Some of the ideas were adapted from Denis Edwards, *Human Experience of God*, p. 27-38 (Paulist Press, 1983).

Tasty and attractive food on the table, produced through a combination of rain and sunshine as well as human effort, witnesses to divine goodness. All these give us a sense of personal smallness contrasted with an almost perceptible awareness of the Mystery beyond.[2]

Secondly, through eyes of faith, one can recognize divine presence in human behaviour – be it the love between a man and a woman, the tenderness of a mother for her baby, the sacrificial devotion of parents to their growing children, or the tireless service of aid workers toward the marginalized living in ill health and extreme poverty in various parts of the world. God's love and grace are perceivable in heroic rescue efforts and selfless sacrifice witnessed after disasters. Volunteers rally and travel long distances to alleviate suffering in areas devastated by hurricanes, tornadoes, earthquakes or tsunamis.

Thirdly, the hand of God may be noticed in our own experiences, often retrospectively. Sometimes tragic events from the past are seen in a new light, and what had appeared as losses is now perceived as great gains. We recognize other special moments of transcendence – something beyond us and outside the ordinary. It can be the chance meeting of a special person who becomes our life partner and soul mate.

---

[2] Psalms 19:1-6 and 65:10; Acts 14:15-17; Romans 1:19-23.

The love shared between friends is likewise something wonderful, undeserved and profound. Experiencing or witnessing the birth of one's own child often gives the parents an overwhelming sense of the mystery of life in which they have been co-creators of a new and unique human being.

Another transcendent moment can be protection when disaster was certain, such as a miraculous avoidance of a car crash. It can also be a special breakthrough, when circumstances came together just at the right time without much effort on our part. Then, there is the inspiration in a creative endeavour – we sense ourselves working in partnership with an outside Source of help, as well as being touched from within, and the final result is more than would have been possible through our own effort. Yet another grace moment occurs when a heart is supernaturally softened and we are enabled to let go of long-held anger and bitterness and to forgive another person who has caused us grievous harm.

Divine grace can also be experienced in fearful situations – such as disaster, terminal illness, tragic death of a loved one, failure and great loss, or abandonment and loneliness. Having exhausted our options and been stretched seemingly beyond our limits, here in our darkest hours we may, perhaps for the first time ever, cry out for help to a Higher Power. And often, there comes a feeling of being upheld, helped and supported. While anguishing to deal with at the time, these experiences may ultimately become life-giving turning points.

And, on day-to-day level, we can intuit divine Providence in delicious food on the table, acts of kindness from loved ones or even strangers, and gracious provision of our needs. Sometimes in the nick of time, we receive desperately needed money, roof over our head, or employment.

Fourthly, divine fingerprints can be found in sacred writings. The Bible, for example, shows God at work in history and in the lives of ordinary individuals. The Old Testament, referred to as the Hebrew Scriptures in the Jewish context, deals primarily with the nations of Israel and Judah descended from the patriarch Abraham (see the books of Genesis through to 2 Chronicles). The history as related in the Scriptures is somewhat based on historical reality, but is also metaphorical – and so has a universal application for life.

In addition, the Word of God provides wisdom principles, as well as examples of human experience in response to God (see, for instance, Psalms, Proverbs, and the book of Job). Prophetically, the Old Testament points to the coming of a Saviour, and ultimately to a restoration of the earth and the universe (see the books of Major Prophets and Minor Prophets).

Camouflage

The New Testament introduces the prophesied Saviour, Jesus Christ, showing how he fulfilled the Old Testament writings and brought salvation to humanity. Jesus also becomes a symbol and embodiment of the Ultimate Reality, which he refers to as his Father. After the death, resurrection, and ascension to heaven of Jesus, the Holy Spirit becomes available by grace to those called to a love relationship with God. Through the Holy Spirit in human hearts and minds, the perception of God increases, Scriptures are opened to understanding, and lives become more kind and loving.[3]

The one transcendent Creator God desires humans to seek and find him. Even though he is incomprehensible and beyond our dimension of existence, he is also not far from any one of us. He does not often communicate in dramatic ways – but rather in a still small voice within, through another person, a special moment or circumstance, or a piece of writing. If we look for and become attuned to these moments of grace in ordinary things and events, we will be amazed and indeed awed at their frequency. It is all a matter of awareness, discernment and perception. Even though God is camouflaged in the

---

[3] Luke 24:25-27, 44-47; John 14:8-11; Acts 1:4-8;1 Corinthians 2:8-16; Galatians 5:22-24; Hebrews 9:28

fabric of life and speaks in quiet whispers, we can become conscious of his very real presence.[4]

---

[4] 1 Kings 19:11-13; Acts 17:27

Birth

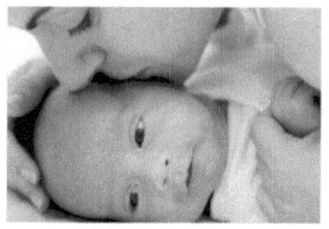 

Jean and Carl bubbled with excitement, joy, and anticipation. Jean couldn't help but tell the whole church congregation, praising God for what had happened. After ten years of marriage, their deepest desire had been realized. A new life had begun inside her – a baby was on the way. Eight months later, a beautiful healthy girl was born. What a miracle!

Sarah and Ben were in a similar situation. They also had trouble conceiving a child that they so desperately desired. Having tried everything medical science had to offer, including artificial insemination, finally, Sarah's pregnancy test came out positive. There too was much rejoicing and hope. In a few short weeks, however, Sarah miscarried and her ecstasy turned into depression. Yet a couple of years later, Sarah gave birth to a boy, and only recently to his brother. She and her husband too feel very blessed.

Prenatal Development

The conception, development and birth of a baby are awe-inspiring. Two microscopic but very different cells (called *gametes* from a Greek word for marriage partners), one from each parent, unite to form the beginning of a new human life – referred to as an embryo, zygote, or *conceptus*. Forty-six chromosomes carry a unique combination of genetic information from both parents. The embryo, however, is far more than a set of instructions for making a new human being. Active and capable of spontaneous growth, the embryo works like several kinds of skilled craftsmen. In the proper order, it constructs the skeleton, muscles, organs, nerve connections, and a waste disposal system for the new body. In a sense, the embryo – already essentially a human being by virtue of the genes – is a blueprint, builder and house combined. In addition to the genetic information, its growth and development is also influenced by its environment – both inside and outside of the mother's body.

Inside the mother, the new life is protected from harm by a fluid-filled sac. Through the placenta – an organ to which the embryo is attached by the umbilical cord – nutrients and oxygen are transferred from the mother's bloodstream and waste products are removed from the baby's. The placenta also produces hormones to maintain the pregnancy, and then to trigger off the birth process through labour in the ninth month when the time has come for the baby to leave the womb.

The human head, body, arms and legs – even hands, feet, fingers and toes – are already formed in the second month of pregnancy, as are the eyes and ears. The cartilage skeleton also turns into bone at this stage and the baby is now called a foetus (from the Greek for young or offspring). From then the organs continue developing until birth when a miniature human being enters the world with its first cry. Those who witness a human birth cannot help but be deeply moved by it. The biblical Psalm 139 expresses the awe of ancient King David, who did not understand prenatal development as we do, yet marvelled at God's incredible handiwork (see v. 14-16).

Spiritual Parallels with Prenatal Development

Prenatal development and birth have many spiritual parallels. In addition to the physical birth resulting in a relatively short life which ends in death, the Scriptures refer to a spirit birth, which leads to eternal, never-ending life. "You must be born again," Jesus told the puzzled Nicodemus, "not of the flesh, but of the Spirit." The apostle Paul describes this phenomenon as "the washing of rebirth and renewal by the Holy Spirit." The Divine Spirit needs to indwell a person – otherwise the individual does not belong to Christ or his kingdom.[5]

The spirit birth is in many ways a mystery and an even greater miracle than the physical birth. But the natural birth can provide a few insights.

The female ovum has a limited life of only about 12 hours and will die unless fertilized by a male sperm. The ovum can be compared to the natural human being – created in God's image, but subject to sin and consequently to inescapable death. Without God's intervention analogous to the fertilizing male sperm, each person is destined to die after a few decades of life without any future hope. Physical conception signifies new life and a new creation, which combines the characteristics of both parents. The spiritual life, imparted by the Holy Spirit, also results in a new creation – with the human parents' characteristics and nature on the one hand and divine nature on the other.[6]

The begotten unborn baby has had nothing to do with the life-giving process. There is no effort and no choice in the matter. None of us chose our parents, time of birth, or whether we will be the first, second, or third of several children. Similarly, a Spirit-

---

[5] John 1:12-13; 3:3-8; Titus 3:5-7; Romans 8:9
[6] Romans 6:4; 8:11-14; 2 Corinthians 5:17; Ephesians 4:22-24; Colossians 3:9-10; 2 Peter 1:4

begotten child of God has no say in the way God chooses to work in their life and nothing to boast about. The whole process is purely God's doing through his love and grace.[7]

Just as an embryo and foetus develop to become more and more like a human being, and specifically his or her parents, children of God acquire more and more of their heavenly Father's characteristics as they grow in relationship with their Lord and Saviour, Jesus Christ. Through the transforming power of the Holy Spirit, they gradually become conformed to the image of God's Son. Over time, the fruit of the Spirit appears – love, joy, peace, patience, kindness, generosity, faithfulness, gentleness and self-control.[8]

The unborn child is already known to the parents, but not yet a visible part of the family. After birth and as they grow, all children reflect more and more of their parents' likeness. God's children, while already possessing seeds of the divine nature and eternal life, are not yet visible in their God-intended glory. As they follow the Spirit's leading and develop spiritual maturity, they are being transformed in mind and character into the image of him who redeemed them from death, called them to himself, justified them,

---

[7] John 1:11-13; 1 Corinthians 1:26-30; Ephesians 2:8-9; 2 Timothy 1:9
[8] Romans 8:29; 2 Corinthians 3:18; Galatians 5:22-23; 2 Peter 3:18

imputed to them his own righteousness, and will glorify them with him at his second coming. At that time, the full adoption or birth into God's family is to take place with "the redemption of the body" – receiving glorious immortal bodies in the resurrection. The children of God will then fully possess divine likeness.[9]

The unborn baby is developing inside the mother's body, attached to her by the umbilical cord through the placenta. The people of God too are growing and developing inside a body – the body of Christ, which is the universal church (not any particular denomination). Moreover, each child of God needs to be individually attached to Jesus Christ. Without this living connection, he or she is likened to a withering branch soon to be broken off. The way the placenta enables nourishment and waste removal or cleansing can be compared to how God through the Scriptures and the Holy Spirit provides nourishment and cleansing for the growing children of God.[10]

The mother carrying the baby inside her where she can best protect it can be compared to God being our protector. He is metaphorically referred to as our refuge, shelter, shield, stronghold, fortress, and strong

---

[9] Romans 8:18, 22-23, 28-30; 12:2; 1 Corinthians 15:42-44, 49; 2 Corinthians 3:18; Philippians 3:20-21; 1 John 3:2
[10] John 15:1-8; 1 Corinthians 12:12-31; Galatians 4:26-31; Ephesians 4:4-7, 11-16; 5:25-32

tower. Furthermore, he sends angels to surround us and protect us from dangers we may not even be aware of.[11]

Unborn children are almost totally unaware of the nature and magnitude of the world outside the womb – a world of which they are unknowingly a part and for which they are preparing. All they register are their parents' muffled voices and a few other sounds. Yet, within very small distance from the wall of the womb, there exists a large dimension, bathed in bright light, of stationary and moving objects with countless shapes, shades and sizes.

In a similar way, the physical life is a preparation for a realm that the Bible says we are not far from, and at the same time, largely unbeknown to us, we are already in it. We have been promised to enter a new dimension of God's kingdom at the resurrection from the dead. While we have an inkling about it, the glory and details of this sphere, that will include and supersede all the dimensions we exist in, are hidden from us and beyond our wildest imagination.[12]

The imminence of physical birth is signalled by the breaking of the waters. The baby no longer needs the amniotic fluid that protected it in the womb since

---

[11] 2 Samuel 22:3, 31; 2 Kings 6:8-17; Psalm 31:2-5; 61:3-4; 91:4-8; Jeremiah 16:19; 17:17

[12] Matthew 4:17; Luke 21:31; Acts 17:26-28; 1 Corinthians 13:12; Ephesians 2:4-7; Hebrews 12: 22-24

conception as it is about to emerge into the world outside the mother's body.

Water plays a symbolic part in the spirit birth. When a person has come to repentance and accepted Jesus Christ as their personal Saviour, he or she is to undergo water baptism. The scriptural example is immersion which symbolizes death and burial of the old self – an identification with Jesus in his death. Emerging out of the water of baptism is a new person in Christ – a new birth has taken place. When Jesus accepted John's baptism and came out of the water, the Holy Spirit visibly descended on him and a voice from heaven affirmed: "This is my beloved son." The symbolism of a new birth or a resurrection as a child of God is central to Christian baptism.[13]

A newborn baby is pure and innocent – not having yet done any evil. It needs to be fed, grow, and learn how to live in its new world. Those of us who have been born again are forgiven and reconciled to God. We stand pure and innocent before our heavenly Father – with Jesus Christ's righteousness having been imputed to us. As babies in Christ, we need to feed on God's Word, grow in grace and knowledge, and be transformed into the image of God by the Holy Spirit (or Christ) living in us. This is the process

---

[13] Matthew 3:13-17; Romans 6:3-6

of sanctification which will continue for the rest of our life on earth.[14]

Special Births

The birth of children is a frequent theme in Scripture. Children are seen as a blessing from God, while barrenness is considered a curse and disgrace. Nevertheless, barren women hold a special place in God's heart, both historically and prophetically. A dramatic reversal of barrenness even symbolizes glorious future salvation of both the people of Israel and the Gentiles.[15]

Several miraculous conceptions and births are recorded of individuals who had a unique role in God's purpose for humanity. Isaac, Jacob (later renamed Israel), Joseph, Samson, Samuel, and John the Baptist were all firstborn miracle babies. Initially their mothers had been unable to conceive naturally, and later these boys were used by God in special ways.[16]

Jesus Christ was a miracle baby in an extraordinary manner, being conceived in Mary by the Holy Spirit, rather than a male sperm. Humanly, we cannot even begin to grasp how one of the members

---

[14] Romans 3:22-24; 5:1-2, 9-10; 8:28-30; 12:1-10; 1 Corinthians 6:11; Colossians 1:19-23; 2 Peter 3:18
[15] Psalms 113:9; Isaiah 54:1-8; Galatians 4:27
[16] Genesis 11:30, Hebrews 11:11-12; Genesis 25:21-26; Genesis 29:31 and 30:22-24; Judges 13:2-24; 1 Samuel 1:5-20; Luke 1:7

of the divine family became God in a human body – both the Son of man and Son of God. Subject to human weakness and tempted in all the ways that we are, yet without sin, he suffered and died for the sins of humanity to be the first to be raised to glory from the dead. Fully human and fully divine, he understands and appreciates what the human experience is all about. How awesome to worship a God, who not only created us, but also can fully identify with us and promises to always be there for us![17]

The Bible speaks of Jesus coming in the flesh – not just the one special time through his birth to Mary, but in an ongoing manner. As through the Holy Spirit God planted Jesus in Mary's womb, after Christ's resurrection and ascension, he has been planting his divine nature through the Holy Spirit in human hearts. A miracle takes place in each case as a person previously unreceptive to God perceives and welcomes divine love and grace.[18]

As the Spirit gently leads the individual to God's Word, to a realization of his or her hopeless condition, to seeing the need for forgiveness and redemption available through Christ's death on the cross, and to a desire for a new life with God leading

---

[17] Luke 2:5-7; Colossians 1:15-20; Revelation 1:5; Romans 8:29; Hebrews 4:15-16, 12:2-3
[18] 1 John 4:2-3; John 14:20; Galatians 2:20; Ephesians 3:16-19; 1 Corinthians 2:9-14

to salvation, the person responds in faith and repentance and receives the down payment of eternal life.[19]

Conversion can indeed be seen as a special divine begettal or birth. Those of us who have experienced it are hidden in God with Christ as a new creation, abide in Christ, are sealed in Christ, experience freedom in Christ, and are able to stand firm in Christ. However, metaphorically, we are also in the process of pregnancy, having Christ formed in us, as well as being transformed into his image.[20]

As representatives or ambassadors of God's kingdom on the earth, we are bringing Christ into the world. As Jesus first came to earth in humility and without fanfare, the kingdom of God is quietly, yet powerfully, entering, and like a small piece of leaven making inroads into Satan's territory. It is not always outwardly visible, but Jesus said that the kingdom of God is within – to perceptibly appear in due time.[21]

The Firstborn

The firstborn is another frequent theme in the Word of God. In the Old Testament, the firstborn child possessed special birthright blessings, being entitled to a double share of the inheritance. Such a

---

[19] Acts 11:18; Colossians 1:27
[20] 1 Corinthians 1:30; 2 Corinthians 1:21; 5:17; Galatians 2:4; 4:19; Ephesians 1:13; 4:13; Colossians 3:3
[21] 2 Corinthians 5:20; Matthew 13:33; Luke 17:20-21

privilege was not to be taken lightly. Esau was rejected from receiving the special blessing because he failed to value it.[22]

The last of the ten plagues before the Exodus brought death to some of the firstborn. All the Egyptian firstborn died, but every Israelite firstborn was protected by blood on doorposts – symbolically redeemed by shed blood. Soon thereafter, God decreed all the male firstborn in Israel, both man and beast, to be his. To perpetually remind the people of the great miracle before leaving Egypt, firstborn animals were to be sacrificed while firstborn sons had to be redeemed.[23]

Like Mary was chosen and especially favoured to become the physical mother of God's Son, those comprising the universal church, the family of God, are also especially selected. The New Testament shows that all who believe become the firstborn children of God and hence heirs of God and co-heirs with Christ. Having responded to God's call in their lives, they are redeemed by Christ's sacrifice on the cross and become a part of the body of Christ, as well as the bride or wife of Christ as the church is also symbolically referred to. If they remain faithful, they are promised to be in the so-called first, or better, resurrection –

---

[22] Deuteronomy 21:15-17; Genesis 25:31-34; Hebrews 12:16-17
[23] Exodus 11:4-7; 12:12-14, 17, 37-42; 13:2,11-16; 34:20

the raising to life of all the dead in Christ. For those in this resurrection, "the second death has no power over them." They are promised special positions in a glorious city full of gold and precious stones where there is absence of tears, suffering and death.[24]

God desires for all to be saved, and the existence of the firstborn and first resurrection implies that others will follow. And indeed, the Scriptures allude to the "rest of the dead" being raised at a later time in a resurrection to physical life. This will include those who by God's design and no fault of theirs were not given the saving grace and knowledge of Jesus Christ during their earthly lives. They will at that time be offered salvation, and if they accept, they will receive the Holy Spirit – the seed of eternal life. While their eternal destiny may be less glorious than that of their firstborn siblings, the wondrous future that God has prepared for all his spiritually born children lies beyond human comprehension and wildest dreams. In the end, God himself will dwell with his people and all things will have been made gloriously new.[25]

---

[24] John 14:2-3; Romans 8:15-18; Ephesians 5:28-32; Hebrews 12:22-23; Revelation 14:1-4; 19:7-9; 20:4-6; 21:1-7

[25] Revelation 20:5, 11-15; 21:1-7; Ezekiel 37:1-14, 20-28

Of Cats, Humans and God

As the employee shopping bus stopped outside our Saudi Arabian block of flats and we unloaded our grocery bags, Ginger, a sand-coloured tabby tomcat, appeared from nowhere. He followed us to the door and obviously wanted something to eat. Having received pieces of cheese in the past, he gradually learned to come whenever he saw us leave or return home – knowing that his affection would be rewarded in kind, in addition to some dry cat food.

We had first seen Ginger up the street near a small private school with a family of cats being looked after by the caretaker. The cats had gotten used to us feeding them, and whenever we walked up the sidewalk, they ran to meet us – sometimes from quite a distance away. Camouflaged in an adjacent desert area, they quickly caught up with us, overtook us, and waited for food on top of one of the round stone seats. Looking up expectantly with trust and devotion, the cats were always rewarded with goodies that I carried in my pocket.

As the weather grew hotter, Ginger took up residence in the garden park across the street. Shady nooks behind benches or cool soil around sprinklers gave him relief from the scorching sun, and water from the fountains quenched his thirst. When he saw or heard us, his appearance was preceded by loud meowing. He would run with a joyous gait, tail to one side, to meet me, then jump onto one of the benches and expect affection and food. As I sat down – having to be careful not to sit on top of him – he snuggled up and contentedly bathed in the loving attention.

Insights from Desert Cats

Most of these cats are descendants of house cats owned by families of embassy employees in the Diplomatic Quarter of Riyadh. When expatriates returned to their home countries, their pets stayed behind and multiplied. While these cats are generally independent and shy, fending for themselves the best way they can, some learn to trust and come to people. Usually, however, it is only because they have been shown kindness first.

A parallel can be seen with us humans. In our natural condition, alienated from God through sin, we tend to fend for ourselves in the deserts of Satan's world. Life is not easy, but somehow we survive, figuratively (and sometimes literally) eating from rubbish bins. Even in this state, however, often without realizing it, we are sustained by a loving God and enjoying the goodness of his universal grace.[26]

In his mercy, God is drawing people to him to be reconciled. Those of us who respond to the divine calling experience God's love and acceptance in a special way. Through the Holy Spirit, our hearts are changed. This tames our independence, although the process of yielding and surrendering to God continues throughout our earthly lives. It is because God has shown us kindness first at some point in our lives that we learn to come to him and trust him.[27]

Having been reconciled to God and as we build a relationship with him, we desire to be close to him and to figuratively snuggle up. We lovingly adore and praise him. Like the cats, however, sometimes we want to, and temporarily do, return to our independent ways. It is not unusual for cats, even house pets, to be gone for two or three days, or even longer, causing worries to their owners. We can act the same way toward our Creator, who redeemed us through Christ's death on the cross. We may be out of sight and hearing for some time, grieving the Holy Spirit.[28]

---

[26] Ephesians 2:12; 2 Corinthians 4:4; 2 Timothy 2:26; Hebrews 2:14; 1 Peter 5:8; Matthew 5:45
[27] 1 Corinthians 1:26-30; 1 Peter 2:9-10; 2 Peter 1:3-4; Jeremiah 31:33; Acts 2:38-39; 2 Corinthians 3:3-6; 1 John 4:10,19
[28] Psalm 103:1-5; Luke 15:11-19; Ephesians 4:22-5:2; 1 Peter 1:18-19

Just as Ginger quickly gets my attention and encouraging response by his meowing, our Heavenly Father is more than ready to respond to our calls and prayers, and welcomes us any time we seek and desire his presence. And while in this earthly life we can seemingly survive on our own – though even here, unbeknown to us, God sustains us – we can have a more joyful and fulfilling life through fellowship and communion with our Maker.[29]

As Ginger comes close and lovingly looks at me, I am reminded of Psalm 42, comparing the deer's panting after water to how we may long for God, the source of living water which symbolizes eternal life. May we desire our independence less and less, and instead seek God's presence as we walk through this desert experience of earthly life. Only in this way will we be able to cross the desert and reach the great river and orchard of everlasting life on the other side.[30]

Individual Differences

After our return from summer vacation, we did not see Ginger for several days, which then stretched into weeks and months. We never found out what happened to him. (Perhaps a new family living in one of

---

[29] Luke 15:20-24; Acts 17:27-28; John 10:9-10
[30] Revelation 22:1-3

the embassy compounds adopted him.) As if to make up for the loss, however, the cat family at the school multiplied. "Mum", as we nicknamed the brown female, had three more kittens before the summer, adding to the other litter of three born earlier in the spring. Each cat had a different and distinct personality.

Of the older litter, White-tip, a ginger cat with white fur at the end of his tail, was a wanderer. He spent his days amidst the rocks in a palm grove area about a kilometre from home. His two siblings, one white and the other ginger and white, were quiet, homely, affectionate cats. They would run from afar to meet us, then run ahead and wait for their titbits at the usual round stone seat. At first, they would share a handful of dry food without a problem. Later, they each needed a separate pile of food, otherwise one would take over and the other miss out.

Among the younger litter, there was Jacob, affectionately named after a very active young boy we got to know. He darted here, there and everywhere, and was unafraid to hit his siblings or even Mum with his small paw and steal their food. Fluffy, a charming long-haired black-and-white tomcat started life on shaky ground. For many weeks, he kept to himself and would not eat. After a time, however, he recovered and grew into a pretty and affectionate cat.

Unfortunately, he later disappeared as well. (Perhaps he stole someone's heart and they took him home with them.) Lastly, Grey, a shy, thin cat, ran away at the slightest sense of danger, be it a passing car, other cats, or people. Her siblings tended to hit her in order to chase her away and eat her food.

At the entrance to our block of flats, Whitey and Blackie became regular visitors. Whitey, a small white female with blue eyes, black tail and loud, piercing meow attracted Blackie, a not particularly pretty or lovable cat, whose request for food came with a hoarse-sounding meow. Both were shy at the beginning, but would eat what we left for them as soon as we were a safe distance away. Sometimes for humanly unknown reasons, Whitey arched her back with hair standing on end, drew her ears back, and growled and hissed at Blackie till he retreated. Even though Blackie was not especially lovable, as we got to know him, we came to like and enjoy him.

Loving All Kinds

Variety in the animal world parallels the uniqueness of each person in families, communities and nations. We vary in colour, habits, thinking and personalities, as well as in ways of relating to each other and to the Divine. Through heredity and environment, some of us seem more lovable than others.

Nevertheless, God knows each of us intimately and works with us in the most suitable and beneficial manner. His immeasurable love embraces every individual, even those whom we may regard as obnoxious.

In fact, since we have all strayed from God and our characters and personalities are stained as a result, none of us is particularly likable. Through wrong (sinful) choices and actions, we have become separated from God and unacceptable to him who is holy. However, through grace beyond measure, God's sinless Son, Jesus Christ, died for the just and the unjust, the lovable and the unlovable. As a result, we have the opportunity to again be accepted by God.[31]

In the way we enjoy watching animals grow, develop, and perform various antics, God takes pleasure in our growth, successes and joys. And, as we feel sad at seeing a sick or injured animal, our caring Heavenly Father also grieves with us when we suffer. He fully understands us, knowing what we are made of, and has great compassion on us in our weakness and foibles. In his omniscience, God knows all about our whereabouts, our needs, and what is best for us. Since he is aware of every bird that falls to

---

[31] Matthew 5:45; Luke 6:35; John 3:16; Ephesians 2:4-9; Romans 5:8-10

the ground, he also knows what happened to Ginger and Fluffy![32]

Seeing kittens growling or hitting each other with their paws is fascinating and amusing. By contrast, when people fall prey to arguing, fighting, or otherwise mistreating each other, this is contrary to God's eternal and timeless *modus operandi* of mutual love. It is not funny as it results in physical and emotional wounds, as well as being destructive to relationships.

However, through a miraculous spiritual rebirth, we can become engaged in a process whereby our hearts are changed from stone to flesh and from hate to love. As a result, our unloving behaviour becomes less and less frequent. And in due time, God will bring about a world where all will live at peace – a world of no war, no hurt, no destruction, no tears, no death, and not even animosity and killing among animals.[33]

Virtue of Stillness and Patience

"Here, puss puss puss!" Tails up, Mum, Jacob and Whitey all come running from under the green gate of the school. Whitey and Jacob leap up onto the stone seat. Mum calmly stays on the ground, rubbing her

---

[32] Psalm 55:22; 103:1-14; Matthew 6:7-8, 32; Luke 12:6-7; 1 Peter 5:7

[33] James 4:1-6; Galatians 5:13-17; Isaiah 2:4; 11:6-9; Ezekiel 36:26-27; John 1:12-13; 3:3-7; Revelation 21:1-4

side against the stone. Jacob, unable to remain still for one moment, keeps jumping up and down from the seat. Whitey lets out a soft meow and looks up expectantly. Mum continues to wait patiently on the ground. When I give each of them in turn a handful of the dry cat food, Jacob pounces on the first portion with his paw. "Don't touch!" is his clear message to Whitey. To make doubly sure, he hits Whitey over the head. Both Whitey and Mum get their food in the next instant even if they don't make any fuss. Finally, all the cats are contentedly eating.

Sometimes all of us can act like Jacob – impatient, intolerant, irritated and quarrelsome. We may want something so badly and urgently, that we figuratively, or even literally, throw a temper tantrum, get nasty with others, fight, or get depressed. We can also get upset or even angry with God. While claiming to want God's will in his time, we get disappointed or unhappy if his will and timing turn out different to ours.

In some ways, Mum epitomizes the fulfilment of two biblical exhortations, namely, to be still and to wait on God. Another way of expressing this is to relinquish our burdens and desires to God – leave the load with him and allow him to resolve the matter in his way and time. There may be a temptation to take the problem back into our own hands or to fret. We need to learn to trust that God is for us and desires the best for each person – that if we knew all the facts and factors, as God does in his omniscience, we would choose the same path that he will eventually lead us to. Of course, these admonitions don't mean adopting a completely passive approach whereby we take no responsible action.[34]

While patience, waiting and trusting do not come naturally, nor are they easy to practice, they will give us peace and serenity in our hearts. If we can relax in faith rather than fret in fear, if we can learn to believe the best rather than expect the worst, and if we can learn to be grateful in all situations, we will find more contentment as our priorities and perspective change. What seemed vital and worthy of endless worry will become relatively insignificant in comparison to the higher realities. Finally, remembering how wonderfully God provided in the past will give us deep trust and confidence towards the future. The words that Moses proclaimed to the Israelites at the edge of the Red Sea with the terrifying Egyptian army in pursuit also apply to us: "Do not be afraid. Stand firm and you will see the deliverance the LORD will bring you

---

[34] Psalm 27:14; 37:1-11; 46:10-11; Proverbs 20:22; 2 Chronicles 20:17; Luke 12:22-32; James 5:7-11

today. ...The LORD will fight for you; you need only to be still."[35]

---

[35] Romans 8:18-25; 2 Corinthians 4:17; Isaiah 30:15-17; Psalm 116:5-9; Ephesians 5:20; Exodus 14:13-14

Pigeons

The small triangular semi-enclosed "balcony" under the window of our Saudi Arabian second-floor apartment must have seemed to them a perfect nesting place. Being fairly high above the ground, shady and hidden, it may have reminded them of a protected cliff place which is the natural habitat of their country relatives. Not just one pair of pigeons wanted to build their home on the balcony, but two pairs literally fought over it – a grey pair and a white pair.

The grey birds found our balcony first and started gathering sticks and other suitable materials for a nest. The male, or cock, brought one stick at a time and placed it in front of his female partner. She then incorporated it into the nest. Their untidy-looking nest was taking shape when the white pair appeared and wanted to settle in the opposite corner. "Too close", decided the grey pair, and the males started fighting. This went on for some time. Several times a day, a bird fight took place, wings flapping or locked around the other bird's neck. Not easily discouraged, the white pair kept returning, while the grey pair kept chasing them away.

While the grey birds built an elaborate nest and the female laid two eggs in it, the white pair managed to put a few sticks together, barely covering the ground in the opposite corner, and to also lay two eggs. However, the war was not over. The grey birds would not allow the white birds to sit on their eggs for long. Pigeon pairs take turns sitting on their eggs – the female does it from late afternoon till mid-morning, while the male does the day shift. So while one of the grey birds sat on the eggs, the other kept the white birds away from theirs. Even though both pairs were persistent, in the end the grey one prevailed. The unhatched eggs were broken, the primitive nest totally dismantled, and any remains of the nest and eggs removed.

After about 18 days, the grey birds' eggs hatched and the parents started taking care of their tiny offspring. Both the male and female pigeons feed their young – producing a cheese-like substance called "pigeon milk", adding seeds and water to the milk, and then regurgitating the mixture into the beaks of the baby squabs. The growing pigeons are fed by the parents for a short time even after they are ready to fly.

Within about four weeks, the baby birds changed from little balls of yellow fluff hidden under the sitting parent to a slightly smaller version of the adult bird. The young birds would stretch their legs and wings on the balcony, but run back into their nest corner whenever they sensed danger. Eventually the day came when they left the nest – now the sticks mixed with and glued together by the birds' droppings, but ready for another set of eggs. Pigeons stay with the same partner for life and may also return to the same nest. They can produce young up to six times a year.

Of Birds and Thoughts

Birds provide an analogy regarding our thought patterns. We cannot stop birds flying over our heads, it is said, but we can stop them from building nests in our hair. In life, we are bombarded with thoughts and ideas all the time – some good, some not. Certain ideas are false and result in deception. The Scriptures show that wrong thoughts and desires, unless rejected, become the seeds or embryos of sin. First, they tempt us, and then lead us into wrong actions, which often bring us trouble or bondage. We may experience unhappy relationships and get into other undesirable situations because of habitual wrong thoughts and attitudes. Thoughts and inner desires are powerful indeed – they can literally shape experiences and circumstances in life. In other words, our thoughts and desires determine what we do and become – what we think makes us what we are.[36]

As our tiny balcony became a battlefield, so is our mind. The two types of birds can be paralleled with thoughts from an invisible, but real enemy – the evil one – and thoughts emanating from God. The evil one is identified in Scripture as Satan the devil – the father of lies who has been allowed to influence earth's inhabitants until the return of Jesus Christ. Godly thoughts come to us through the Holy Spirit. Unwittingly, all of us have been conditioned by the devil's lying thoughts and deception prevalent in this world. False beliefs can take such deep roots, that they become strongholds over which we feel powerless. They can be like the white birds – persistent and not giving up easily, even to the point of "nest building."[37]

What to do? In this battle for the mind, God proides us with spiritual weapons, and the Bible gives helpful principles on how to use them.[38]

---

[36] James 1:13-15; Proverbs 23:7 (KJV); Romans 8:5; Luke 11:39-44
[37] John 8:44-45; Ephesians 2:1-3; 6:12
[38] Ephesians 6:13-18; 2 Corinthians 10:4-5. Some of the following ideas were adapted from Joyce Meyer, *Battlefield of the Mind: How to Win the War in Your Mind* (Harrison House, 1995)

Firstly, realize that only the truth of Christ will set you free from deception and error and enable you to live fruitfully.[39]

Secondly, learn to take responsibility for your life rather than searching for someone or something to blame. (Blaming others has been a proclivity of humans from the beginning of time.[40])

Also, accept that courage is needed to change because making changes is never easy. Ask God for help and then trust him to strengthen you and to provide a way.[41]

Next, build a daily habit of prayer, Bible study and meditation, and let the divine Word and the Holy Spirit transform your mind little by little into the mind of Christ.[42]

Boldly claim God's promise to supply wisdom when you need it, and to have the Spirit intercede on your behalf when you don't know how to pray about a situation.[43]

Continue to be patient and fight the temptation to give up, knowing that God will complete his work that he has begun in you.[44]

---

[39] John 8:31-32; Romans 8:1-2
[40] Genesis 3:1-13
[41] Joshua 1:9; 1 Corinthians 10:13; 1 Peter 5:10
[42] Matthew 4:4; Luke 18:1; Romans 12:2; Joshua 1:8; cf. Deuteronomy 7:22
[43] James 1:5-8; Romans 8:26-27
[44] Luke 8:15; Philippians 1:6, 2:12-13

Finally, strive to stay faith-filled and positive, think edifying thoughts, and expect good things.[45]

Knowing how powerfully thoughts, perceptions and beliefs influence our life, we need to discern between wrong thoughts luring us away from God (eventually making us feel desolate), and right thoughts leading us into faith, hope and love (bringing us comfort). As we mindfully reflect on our thinking patterns and examine our beliefs, we are likely to recognize which particular thoughts and ideas cause us problems and make us unhappy. When we understand this, we can be like the grey birds on the balcony in fighting the wrong kind of thinking – determined, persistent, vigilant, and never giving up. In this way, with divine help, over time, we will gain victory.[46]

A New Generation of Pigeons

The last pair of young pigeons left the nest a few months ago. Some activity on our small balcony had continued, including an occasional fight, but no eggs. White birds and grey birds wandered on the balcony ledges, chased another bird away, rested for a while, and flew off again. I wondered if the now solid nest consisting of twigs, droppings and feathers was going

---

[45] Proverbs 15:13, 15; Philippians 4:8
[46] 2 Corinthians 13:5-6; Romans 8:37; 1 Peter 5:8-10; 1 Corinthians 15:57-58; 1 John 5:4-5

to be used again. Then, one day, an egg appeared. A day or two later, another egg. After that a white pigeon came to sit on the nest.

Over the next few days, I discovered that the white bird's partner was grey. As a general, rule, the white female bird sat on the eggs till about 10 am and the grey one took its place thereafter. Sometimes the white bird remained till about 2 pm and the grey one came for an afternoon shift. At daybreak, the white bird was usually back.

Even though no competitor tried to settle in the opposite corner of the balcony, occasional savage fights still occurred. Another bird would come and challenge the egg sitter, and the two would fight fiercely, sometimes for half an hour or more. Occasionally a three-bird fight took place – the owners of the eggs against the intruder. They hit each other with their wings and pecked one another on the head and neck so hard that blood appeared.

The white birds are white because they have no pigment in their feathers. They appear extra beautiful, clean and special, and have been used as peace symbols. After several fights in the dust and dirt of the balcony, however, the white pigeon looked dirty and had a few drops of blood on its white feathers.

Impressive to me was the undeterred patience with which the birds sat on their eggs. Apart from chasing away or fighting with intruders, the birds sat still for hours, keeping the eggs warm and waiting for the young to hatch. After that, they sat on the babies, each parent for about half of each 24-hour period. Also when it rained, the parent birds faithfully protected the young chicks. With heavier rain, the little balcony gradually filled with water and the birds would get wet, but they still remained. Only a movement in the adjacent window, such as opening it, caused them to fly away for a short while, but soon they returned. Luckily, the nest was high enough for the eggs and young birds to remain dry. A past generation of young pigeons whose nest was smaller drowned when a downpour came.

One rainy day, I noticed only one young chick in the nest, and it was alone – no parent in sight. Had something happened to the adult bird? A number of cats lived in the neighbourhood – did the pigeon become dinner for one of them? Was there another reason the birds had deserted the nest? I also wondered what happened to the other chick. The poor remaining chick was getting soaked and I felt sorry for it. Finally, the grey bird appeared and sat on the nest – I am sure, much to the relief of the cold, drenched baby bird.

As time went on, the young growing bird was left alone for longer periods. The parents showed up for short stretches of time, gave it food, but did not stay long. Day by day, the young bird grew bigger, stronger, and more active. The only difference in appearance from the adult bird was a bit of yellow fluff on its head. Instead of just sitting in the nest, it started running around and flapping its wings. Then, one day it flew up to the lower balcony ledge and, after some hesitation, back down again. A few days later, it made it up to the window sill. Both parents started appearing more often – perhaps to encourage their chick in its flying attempts. Finally, the bird reached the higher balcony ledge – with both parents on either side of it. Next, it was gone – having made its maiden flight from two floors above ground. The parents were also gone, but soon they returned.

The young bird would not have been ready to face the tough world yet – to find its own food and mate, and to start the cycle of life all over. This was just the beginning of its real-life education. The parents stayed on the higher balcony ledge, looking down, the male cooing, presumably calling the chick. When other birds responded to the cooing, they were promptly chased away. The parents spent their time on the ledges and in the nest – perhaps not unlike human parents anxiously awaiting the return of their teenage son or daughter from the first night out. At one point, the female even sat on top of the male on the nest as if to comfort him that the youngster would be all right. I wondered, can the inexperienced chick fly back up to the balcony before a cat below has it for a meal? Have the parents misjudged how high up the nest is?

But yes, about four hours later, the chick made it back. It seemed a sign for mother that it no longer needed to be fed by her. She resisted the chick's squeaking and efforts to get food out of her beak. The male bird arrived later. In response to its squeaking, he gave the chick some food, but only a little. The young bird was being weaned and taught to look after itself.

For the next few weeks, between the young bird's flights, both parents spent time on the balcony with the chick. Sometimes they were looking at the nest as if to reminisce on days gone by. The ever-hungry chick never ceased to try to get food from one or the other parent, sometimes successfully, sometimes not. I assume that it had to catch its own meal when the parents refused to cooperate. Finally the day came when the whole pigeon family was gone.

Other Analogies

In the Scriptures, white signifies righteousness, light and truth. The children of God are symbolically dressed in white, having Christ's righteousness imputed to them. However, like the white pigeon defending its nest and getting dirty and bloodied in the process, we too face an ongoing struggle with wrong thoughts and choices that stain our spiritual garments. In church history, and even presently in certain parts of the world, some have become literally bloodied, or even martyred, for defending their way of life. Through it all, the Holy Spirit – the Comforter, Counsellor or Advocate – comforts and strengthens us, and Christ's blood shed on the cross cleanses us again and again upon expressing regret for our failings and desiring to change.[47]

Despite an ongoing struggle between good and evil, truth and goodness will ultimately prevail. With the previous pigeon occupants on the balcony, the grey pair (for our purposes, considered symbolically evil) gained victory over the white birds (symbolically righteous). Sometimes this happens in real life, at least for a time. In the world, both historically and presently, evil individuals overpower the just. Ungodly and unjust laws are passed, evil deeds are sanctioned, and the innocent suffer. Prophetically, the antichrist overcomes the saints.

This however does not represent the end of the story. Even though the state of the present world is getting worse, God's Word foretells a dramatic reversal in global trends with the supernatural return of

---

[47] Revelation 3:4; 19:7-9; Ephesians 6:10-18; Hebrews 9:14; 11:35-40; 12:1-4; John 14:16-18, 26; 1 John 1:7

the Son of God to earth. In the end, all evil will be overcome and removed.[48]

Like the adult pigeons patiently waiting for their young to hatch, grow up and mature, we too are exhorted to patience – waiting for our Lord who promised to return and give us immortality. Through biblical revelation and the eyes of faith, we seek to keep the blessed hope burning in our hearts. If our life ends before the return of the Deliverer, we can be confident in the promise of resurrection from the sleep of death and being with our Saviour and Redeemer for all eternity.[49]

While waiting implies patience, it doesn't mean passivity. We have a mission – the Lord's work means being ambassadors for Christ and bringing hope to a world where many are alienated from their Creator and live contrary to the divine way of peace and love. Although we must live in the world, our citizenship and allegiance are in the kingdom of heaven. Not being of the world, we need to resist being weighed down by its cares and absorbing its false values.[50]

At times, God leaves us seemingly alone in the "cold and rain", just like the pigeon parents left their young one. Yet, in his immanence, God is never far.

---

[48] Jeremiah 12:1-2; Psalms 73:1-28; Revelation 12:9-12; 13:4-7; 17:12-14; 19:1-6
[49] Titus 2:11-15; 1 Thessalonians 4:13-17; 1 Corinthians 15:51-57
[50] Luke 19:12-26; 2 Corinthians 6:14-18; James 1:27; 2 Corinthians 5:19-21; Philippians 3:20-21

Even though we cannot see him and may not even sense his presence, he has promised to never leave nor forsake us. As we mature spiritually, God may not be answering our prayers as he used to. When we experience a "dark night of the soul", facing God's silence in response to our petitions, he is actually helping us to develop a purer faith, trust and patience. In his omniscience, God always knows how much we can handle and promises never to test us more than we can endure. Also, he will not do for us what we can do for ourselves, and fully expects us to do what we are ready and able to do.[51]

Regardless of surrounding appearances and personal challenges, we are encouraged to walk by faith, not by sight – and to thereby live above our circumstances. After all, God has given us breathtaking promises and assurances. Someone once quipped: "I have looked at the end of the book, and we win." At that time, all the suffering now experienced will be hardly worth mentioning in the perspective of eternity and the future glory.[52]

---

[51] Acts 17:27; Hebrews 13:5-6; James 1:2-4; 1 Peter 1:6-9; 1 Corinthians 10:13
[52] 2 Corinthians 4:17; 5:4-6; Romans 8:16-18

Insights from Frogs

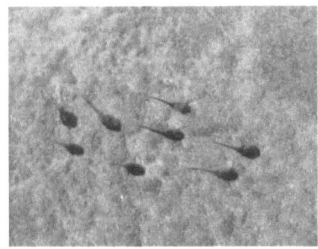 

The shallow pool teemed with hundreds of black tadpoles. The smaller ones were attached to the bottom or sides of the pool, or to submerged plants, while the bigger ones swam around, propelling themselves through the water by their tails. Before too long, they will develop at first back legs, then front legs, as well as lungs. They will also lose their tails and take on the likeness of adult frogs. When that happens, they will not be restricted only to water, but will be able to live on land and breathe air. An amazing transformation will have taken place within a short span of 14-16 weeks.

Frog Life Cycle

The life cycle starts with the male and female frogs mating. The female lays thousands of eggs, which the male fertilizes as they are laid. The eggs are laid either in still water or above it, so that when they hatch, the tadpoles will not be buffeted and carried away by water currents. Out of the large mass, however, only a comparatively few of the eggs are fertilized, hatch, survive, and develop into adult frogs.

Fertilization imparts life to the egg. An unfertilized egg will stay alive for only a very short time and not grow or develop in any way. The fertilized frog egg soon starts dividing into multiple cells which differentiate into body parts such as the mouth, tail, and internal organs. When the tadpole hatches, it lives of the egg yolk, which is in its gut.

Initially, tadpoles remain attached to surfaces in the water. As they grow, they start swimming around and feeding on algae. Gradually, they develop small teeth and their diet also includes plants and dead insects. By about four weeks of age, they may join other tadpoles in schools.

The process in the frog life cycle is a gradual metamorphosis – imperceptible from day to day, but clearly visible over a period of time. As the tadpole matures, it goes through stages of having both tadpole and frog characteristics. It starts developing back legs and lungs, but retains its long tail. Later, front legs appear, coming out "elbows" first, and the tail shortens.

The tadpole is restricted to water. It uses gills and is unable to breathe air until it develops lungs. Adult frogs can live both in water and on dry land. The transforming tadpole stage, lasting 3-4 months, is relatively short compared to the frog's adult life of several years.

Spiritual Parallels

Analogies can be seen between the tadpole's metamorphosis into a frog and our transformation into the likeness of Christ.

The frog lays thousands of eggs, but only a comparatively few of them are fertilised, hatch, survive, and develop into adult frogs. A similarity is expressed in the biblical concept of "many are called, but few are chosen." When the Word of God is publicly disseminated, it is like seed being sown. However, not all of the seed will germinate and produce fruit. Some who hear the message of salvation – the gospel – neglect it due to the cares of the world, desires for pleasures and riches, trials and persecution, or deception of Satan.[53]

Without being fertilized, an egg will survive for only a very short time. In a sense, each human being is like an unfertilized egg – here for just a few decades, ending in death and disintegration. The

---

[53] Matthew 20:16; 22:14; Matthew 13:18-23; Mark 4:14-20; Luke 8:13-15

Scriptures compare the human life to short-lived vapour or grass.[54]

The fertilization process can be compared to the germ of eternal life imparted by God through the Holy Spirit. The divine Spirit unites with the human spirit and is instrumental in the transformation into divine likeness. Upon Christ's return, it will also be the key factor in bringing about a resurrection from the dead to life eternal.[55]

When the tadpole hatches, it lives for a time of the egg yolk, which is in its gut. The life-giving Spirit first starts working internally – in the heart and mind, providing spiritual nourishment. Slowly, almost imperceptibly, our perspective changes and we become receptive to the things of God, in which of and by themselves, without divine intervention humans are not interested. We gain new understanding of life, and spiritual matters start making sense as our eyes are opened. This is the first step in the Spirit's transformation.[56]

As they grow, tadpoles start feeding on algae and when their teeth develop, their diet also includes plants and dead insects. They also join other tadpoles in schools. In a similar manner, new Christians need

---

[54] James 1:9-11; 4:13-15
[55] Romans 8:9-16
[56] John 6:44, 65; 14:16-17, 26; Luke 24:25-32; 1 Corinthians 2:9-14

an easily digestible spiritual diet before becoming ready for solid food. Additionally, we all need a spiritual community and fellowship, which we receive through the body of Christ – the church.[57]

The female frog laid her eggs either in still water or above it, so the young tadpoles wouldn't be buffeted and carried away by water currents. Through the ministries in the church, God provides for his children still water and spiritually calm conditions. It is in the world that we encounter turbulent circumstances. Jesus tells us "in me you may have peace", whereas "in this world you will have trouble". But even then, help and a way of escape are promised.[58]

The Transformation

The process in the frog's life cycle is a gradual metamorphosis – imperceptible from day to day, but clearly visible over a period of time. So it is with our transformation into Christ's likeness. We are often unaware that we are slowly changing through the gentle renewal of our minds by the Holy Spirit, but when we look back on our life, we see an undeniable change in our thinking, perspective and interests.[59]

---

[57] 1 Corinthians 3:1-3; 1 Peter 2:1-3; Hebrews 5:12-14; 10:23-25
[58] Psalm 23:1-2; Ephesians 4:11-14; John 16:33; 1 Corinthians 10:13
[59] Romans 12:2; 2 Corinthians 3:18; 4:16; Ephesians 4:20-25; Colossians 3:9-11; Titus 3:5-7

The tadpoles are restricted to water while adult frogs can live both in water and on dry land. As humans, we are restricted to planet Earth. For a short time, a few individuals have ventured into space, but without sophisticated equipment providing for them what the Earth provides, they would not survive long. Jesus Christ, our forerunner as the firstborn from the dead, has transcended earthly existence. After his resurrection, he could appear and disappear through walls, doors, or other physical barriers. On resurrection Sunday, he ascended to the Father and returned on the same day. We are promised to fully bear his image and receive bodies with the same abilities. While we will be able to spend time on the Earth, we will not be bound to it.[60]

The maturing tadpole goes through stages of having both tadpole and frog characteristics. Christians, in developing their Lord's likeness, also possess two natures – the human and the divine. These two natures may conflict with each other, pulling us towards sinful desires on the one hand and the things of God on the other. To reach our destiny through the resurrection from the dead, we must choose and pursue that which fosters the spiritual nature, and thereby subdue the wrong inclinations.[61]

---

[60] John 20:16-26 and Matthew 28:1-9; 1 Corinthians 15:41-49
[61] Romans 7:18-25; 8:12-14; Colossians 3:1-5; Philippians 3:8-14; 2 Peter 1:4

The adult frog lives in two worlds – water and dry land. In some ways, we also live in two worlds. Physically, we are bound to the Earth, where Satan still exerts considerable influence. Spiritually, however, because of Christ's sacrifice on the cross, we have access to "heavenly places" through prayer and meditation. We live in the world, but as ambassadors of Christ no longer desire to participate in ungodly practices and customs – in other words, we are in the world, but not of it. And, while we have various nationalities on the Earth, our real citizenship is in heaven.[62]

The transforming tadpole stage lasts only a few short months compared to the frog's adult life of several years. Likewise, our earthly life, during which we are progressively transformed into Jesus Christ's likeness, is very short compared to eternity.

Initially, a tadpole looks nothing like an adult frog. As it develops, however, more and more similarities appear, though differences remain until the final stage. Before the indwelling divine Spirit starts to transform us into Christ's image, our ego-driven nature can make us very unlike God. Nevertheless, with time, more and more similarities appear till

---

[62] Ephesians 1:3,15-21; 2:1-7; John 12:31; 14:30; 15:19; 17:15-16; Matthew 5:14; 1 Corinthians 2:12; 2 Corinthians 4:4; James 4:4; 1 John 2:16; Philippians 3:20-21

finally, in the resurrection, we will receive the full likeness of Christ.[63]

While all analogies are imperfect and limited, they can be helpful in allowing us to better visualize realty. The next time we spot tadpoles swimming in a puddle or a frog hopping around at the water edge, perhaps we will briefly reflect on the marvel of their, and our own, transformation.

---

[63] 1 Corinthians 15:49; 1 John 3:1-2

Butterfly Metamorphosis

The small blue butterflies gracefully hovered over the young shoots of the cycad (trunkless plant with palm-like leaves). While I knew it spelled trouble for the new shoots, the fragile, gentle, seemingly defenceless creatures fascinated me.

Butterflies come in various colours, shapes and sizes. Watching the flight of a colourful butterfly from flower to flower cannot help but elicit a sense of awe and wonder. Our marvel may increase as we reflect on where the beautiful butterfly came from – a clumsy, earthbound caterpillar that during its maturing stages can be highly destructive. And yes, the tender shoots of the cycad were indeed devoured by the caterpillars hatched from the eggs laid by the blue butterflies.

It's not surprising that the transformation of an unsightly crawling caterpillar into a strikingly beautiful airborne butterfly has been seen in spiritual terms – such as a symbol of the transfiguration of the human soul at death. Indeed, analogies can be drawn between the transformation that occurs in the life cycle of a butterfly and the spiritual destiny of humanity as alluded to in the Holy Scriptures.

Life Cycle of a Butterfly

A butterfly life cycle consists of four basic stages – egg, caterpillar (larva), pupa (chrisolis), and adult butterfly. Only a small percentage of the eggs develop into a butterfly because of the complexity of the process and the numerous dangers along the way. Nonetheless, the transformation from a caterpillar to butterfly is awe-inspiring.

The life cycle begins with the mating of a male and female of the same species. In some species, males and females look very similar. There are also similarities between butterflies of unrelated species, therefore finding a suitable partner is a challenge.

In the process of mating, the male passes to the female a package containing sperm as well as nutrients for the eggs and for the female herself – a so-called "nuptial gift". This essential package, created over a period of time, can have up to half the weight of the butterfly.

After mating, the female must locate an appropriate host plant in a place with favourable conditions – another complex course of action. She then lays eggs on a leaf (or another suitable surface) that will supply food to the offspring once they have hatched.

In about five days, the caterpillars (larvae) emerge and start feeding, quickly increasing in size. Caterpillars consume huge amounts of plant food and can leave a bush or a tree bare. They grow at an almost exponential rate and are able to gain over 3000 times their original weight!

As it grows, each caterpillar sheds its skin (molts) several times. The periods between molts are called *instars*, and each instar may be characterized by a different appearance. At the end of the last instar, the caterpillar turns into a pupa.

During the last instar phase and the time in the pupa, a period of several weeks, a complete reorganization of body parts takes place. The caterpillar body is dissolved and a butterfly body is assembled from previously undifferentiated cells – an astounding marvel of nature. At the end of this period, the pupa splits and the butterfly is almost ready to start its new life. Before it can fly, however, the wings need to be expanded by pumping body fluid through the veins. The fluid is then withdrawn so that the wings can dry. Only then is flight possible.

While the caterpillar grew phenomenally, the butterfly does not grow. Its main functions are to pollinate flowers and to reproduce. It needs quality food, however, to have sufficient energy for flying. In contrast to the caterpillar stage, the butterfly also has excellent sensory capabilities – sight, smell and touch.

A great variety in appearance, lifestyle and behaviour exists among the eggs, caterpillars, pupae and butterflies of the more than 18,000 butterfly species. Diversity is found even within the same species living in different areas. Butterflies also have complex relationships with other creatures and the environment.

These extraordinary creatures have fascinated humanity for millennia. The ancients saw butterflies as symbols of the psyche, soul, mind, resurrection and purity. The next section examines from a biblical perspective and personal reflections how this remarkable insect can give us insights into the human life and our destiny beyond this life.

Physical and Spiritual Parallels

The butterfly life cycle starts with the male, in the process of mating, giving the female a "nuptial gift" – a provision for her and the offspring. This can be compared to the gift of the Holy Spirit we receive upon conversion when we come into union with the Divine. The Spirit provides for our spiritual needs and guarantees our future resurrection – or "butterfly emergence".[64]

---

[64] John 14:20; 17:23; Acts 2:38; 10:45; Romans 8:11, 26; Philippians 1:19; Colossians 1:27

The egg stage can be compared to human conception and birth. Every person starts as a fertilized ovum (or egg). Just as the female butterfly provides a place for its offspring where food is abundant, the human embryo and then foetus is fed and nurtured inside the mother where it grows and develops sufficiently to be born into the world.

The rapidly growing caterpillar stage, comprising a number of sub-stages (instars) separated by molts or skin shedding, may represent this earthbound life consisting of several distinct stages – infancy, childhood, adolescence, adulthood and old age. Rapid physical growth and development occur in the early stages. During adulthood, we grow in wisdom, kindness and compassion.[65] With growth, maturing and aging, appearance also changes.

The caterpillar goes through several stages of transformation during its lifespan. Interestingly, it is able to slow down or delay going from one stage to the next – a phenomenon called *diapause*. As humans, we are intended to grow and become transformed by the renewing of our mind. Yet, not unlike the caterpillar, we can resist making needed changes to which we are led by God, other people, or circumstances.[66]

---

[65] 2 Chronicles 10:6-11; Job 32:6-9
[66] 2 Peter 3:18; Romans 12:1-2; Ephesians 4:22-27, 30; Acts 7:51; 1 Thessalonians 5:19

The caterpillar stage can be very destructive in that whole trees and bushes may be denuded and even killed. History shows how humans can also be greedy and destructive to their environment.

This stage of the butterfly life cycle faces many dangers and obstacles, such as being eaten by predators, becoming a source of food for the larvae of parasitoids that lay their eggs inside the caterpillar, or failing to get to another food source after exhausting the previous one. To compensate for its vulnerabilities, the caterpillar has multiple survival strategies, which include camouflage, warning colours to deter predators, or a silken thread on which it can drop off of a leaf and thus escape.

While at times some of us may feel invincible, human life too is fragile and can be quickly and unexpectedly snuffed out. Our defences include using knowledge and wisdom to avoid (as much as possible) dangerous situations. The Scriptures also describe spiritual defence apparatus for our use – the Holy Spirit and "the armour of God". Additionally, we are promised a way of escape when a situation becomes too difficult to bear – a spiritual version of the silken thread.[67]

Differences exist in appearance, lifestyles and behaviour among and even within the thousands of

---

[67] Ephesians 6:11-18; 1 Corinthians 10:13

butterfly species. The same is true of humanity. While we are all of one species, we too differ in appearance, lifestyles and behaviour. And, like butterflies, we also have a complex relationship with our environment, including the plant kingdom and other living creatures.

Unlike butterflies, we are not programmed by instinct to successfully deal with one another and other species, but rather given free will and the accompanying responsibility to choose our attitude and behaviour toward others and our surroundings. If we fail to act in respect, love and tolerance toward fellow humans, other creatures, and the environment, we inevitably bring problems and potential disaster on ourselves and others.

During the last instar and the pupal stage, a reorganization of body parts occurs – the caterpillar parts disintegrate and new butterfly parts are formed. The pre-pupal stage can be compared to our aging – time when some of our body processes cease and we lose certain capabilities due to degeneration of organs. The pupal stage can be analogous to physical death – a cessation of life as we know it, characterized by such activity as physical movement, food intake, elimination, and thought processes. A disintergration of the physical body occurs over time – where ultimately it ends as dust.

The Scriptures reassure us, however, that there is hope beyond death. They speak of a future resurrection to a new, eternal, life – which on the one hand may have similarities with this life, yet also be very different. Like the butterfly compared to the caterpillar, we will transcend our earthbound existence – and then greatly exceed what can be done through modern technology, have far more highly developed senses, and achieve exceedingly more than we could have ever dreamt.

Jesus Christ is the pioneer of our salvation and the Bible gives us glimpses of our next life if we look at his. We will have a new and glorious body – the same type of body that Jesus has had since his resurrection. Our future appearance will be like his – we shall see him as he is, for we shall be like him. He could appear and disappear at will, transcend physical barriers, and manifest in glory – with his face and body shining as the brightness of the sun. He could foresee events and knew what people were thinking. We will no longer be selfish and destructive, but rather, like Jesus, abounding in love, kindness and grace. [68]

---

[68] Philippians 3:21; 1 Corinthians 15:43-44; Luke 24:13-43; Revelation 1:12-18; 1 John 3:2

Butterfly Metamorphosis

Quoting butterfly researcher, Jo Brewer[69]: "The science of butterflies is neither dull nor dogmatic. It is like the unfolding of a mystery, the ending of which is not known until the last page is turned." The same is true of life – we will not know its ultimate outcome till we reach the final stage. Until then, may we each follow the Holy Spirit in working out our salvation, looking in faith and hope to the time when our metamorphosis is complete and when, like the butterfly, we will transcend this earthbound existence and be able to soar to new, previously undreamt of heights.[70]

---

[69] Jo Brewer is a co-author with her husband, Dave Winter, of *Butterflies and Moths – A Companion to Your Field Guide* (Phalarope Books) and author of other books on butterflies.
[70] Philippians 2:12-16; Galatians 5:22-25; Romans 8:13-17, 28-32; Ephesians 1:13-14

Emperor Penguins

Antarctica is an exceptionally inhospitable environment. The long winter consists of six dark, cruel months without the sun being as much as sighted, temperatures going down to minus 40 to 60 degrees Centigrade, winds of up to 200 kilometres per hour, and fierce blizzards further increasing the chill factor. There is a short period of milder weather, but still harsh living conditions. Despite all this, life not only exists there, but is able to thrive.

The life cycle of the emperor penguin is an amazing story of communal living, partner cooperation, bearing one another's burdens, personal sacrifice, patient endurance, and making the most of opportunities. Having a life span of 20 years or more, feeding on small sea life gotten from 150 to 250 metres below the surface, and reproducing from the age of four onward in extremely difficult circumstances, the penguin is a marvel of design. Much can be learnt from these incredible birds.

Penguin Life Cycle

The cycle starts at the end of summer, March/April, when the penguins travel 50 to 120 kilometres from the sea to their inland breeding grounds. Not having wings to fly, they walk the distance or slide on their bellies on downhill slopes – both modes of ambulation being quite comical.

Upon arrival at the old breeding grounds, a short courtship starts. Each male uses a unique sound to call a female, and before long, there is pairing. Penguin males remain with the same partner for the whole breeding season, and if they find her the following year, they will pair off again. Often they do not find the same partner, so they pair off with another bird.

After mating, each female lays a single egg, which she quickly and skilfully transfers to the male. The father balances it on his feet and immediately covers it with his brood pouch. Both the male and female birds have a pouch above their feet where they keep their egg, and later baby chick, from freezing. Without this protection, neither the egg nor the tender hatchling would survive in the extremely frosty conditions.

Following the journey, mating and egg laying, the females are exhausted and need to quickly return to the sea to feed. They must yet travel 50 to 80 kilometres to get there. While their partners are gone for the rest of the winter, the males incubate the eggs under extremely harsh conditions. It is an example of marvellous adaptation, as well as cooperation between the male and female and their well-defined roles. While one feeds to survive and to bring food, the other looks after the offspring.

When the females leave, the males all huddle together in a turtle-shaped formation to keep as warm as possible. They take turns inside and outside of the huddle, giving everyone a chance to warm up as well as protect the others from the cruel elements. For 65 days, the fathers, each with an egg on his feet, stand without eating, huddled together in freezing temperatures, gale force winds, and blinding blizzards. They sleep as much as possible to conserve energy.

As the sun returns from the northern hemisphere to bring light to Antarctica, it also brings with it life from the sea, including hundreds of female penguins. They are coming to the rescue of their partners. Each will recognize their mate by his characteristic call. The eggs have now hatched and the females are ready to take care of the young chicks, freeing the males to get some food after their four-month abstinence. The females have food stored in their stomachs to feed the young, while the males will travel 50 or more kilometres to the open sea to replenish their reserves.

When the chick hatches, the father provides one meal for it that keeps it going for several days till the mother arrives. Even though the father's stomach is empty after months of no food intake, he has a throat-sac which secretes emergency nourishment for the chick in the form of a milky, protein-rich substance.

Upon being reunited with his partner, the male quickly transfers the young bird from his pouch to that of the mother. She then feeds it regurgitated food in the pouch till it is bigger, otherwise, outside the pouch it would freeze to death in a couple of minutes. When the chicks are strong enough to withstand the weather, they are left by the parents in colonies called crèches, while the adults go searching for food.

By December, some of the ice breaks up enabling both young and adult penguins to go to the open sea. They spend the summer diving and fishing, replenishing their reserves for another harsh winter. Penguins feed on small sea food and go to considerable depths – 150 to 250 or more metres below the surface – to find it. They can hold their breath for up to 20 minutes, making several dives in that time.

This period of abundance doesn't last long – in three or four months it nears its end. Penguins that are old enough to breed start another pilgrimage inland to the breeding grounds, while those too young to reproduce stay at the sea. Emperor penguins are the only animals that remain in Antarctica in winter and breed on the open ice. Driven by incredibly programmed instinct, their internal clock tells them when it is time to assemble and start moving as a community. At the breeding grounds, they will again pair off and the whole cycle will be repeated.

Penguins have a tremendous ability to endure hardship. Not only can they withstand the extreme cold, but they can also go without food for months on end, travel long distances in adverse conditions, and obtain their food from great ocean depths. Their endurance appears to be stretched to the limit – any longer before relief comes and it might be too late. For example, the female lays the egg and has just enough energy to make the distance to the sea to feed. The males have endured a gruelling winter season without eating when the females return and free them up to start a journey back to the sea to get desperately needed nourishment.

Spiritual Parallels

The fascinating life story of emperor penguins in some ways parallels the Christian journey. This section draws a number of comparisons.

Penguins spend considerable time travelling back and forth between the sea and their breeding grounds. Since they are unable to fly, this is no small journey. The Christian life is a pilgrimage or journey, symbolized by the biblical story of the exodus from Egypt to the Promised Land. It consists of good seasons as well as times of adversity, abundance as well as scarcity. It is an odyssey requiring endurance. Sometimes we may feel like the penguins waddling and sliding, going back and forth, learning and relearning lessons. But upon careful reflection, we'll notice a divine hand working behind the scenes for our benefit.[71]

Pairing is the result of the male bird using a special call to attract a female. Once she responds, the two remain together for the whole season, even though they need to separate for a time in order to survive. Jesus Christ sends out a call to attract those that his Father is drawing to him. These people recognize his voice, respond, and become his forever. They enter a lifelong relationship with Jesus and become attuned to his distinct voice among all the other luring voices in the world. When Christ returns, he will again call, and this time his people will respond and rise from their graves to be with him forever.[72]

Male penguins survive the cruel winter only because of staying together as a community and helping each other. They keep one another warm and take

---

[71] Psalm 78:12-41,52-55; Philippians 3:7-14; Hebrews 12:1-3
[72] John 10:11-16, 27; 5:25-28; 1 Thessalonians 4:16-17; Job 14:14-15

turns bearing the brunt of the winds and blizzards, exemplifying personal sacrifice and patient endurance. We also need a community for our protection and spiritual survival. This is the body of Christ – the church. We are exhorted not to forsake regular assembling and fellowship. In addition we are to love one another, live together in unity, and bear one another's burdens. Just like the penguins, we need each other and cannot survive by ourselves.[73]

Amazing cooperation exists between the male and female as they alternate in taking care of their offspring and providing food for themselves. The males also sacrifice a great deal as they incubate the egg in the worst of weather.

Good marriages exemplify successful cooperation of the partners helping one another and caring for their offspring. The ideal husband typifies Jesus Christ in loving and serving his wife, while she willingly submits to his servant leadership. When children arrive, both parents do their best for their welfare. They can most help their offspring to have successful lives by setting an example of mutual love, respect, and submission. The ancient King Solomon, known for his wisdom, stated that two are better than one. However, in contrast to penguins that have been programmed to know exactly what to do and when,

---

[73] John 17:20-23; Galatians 6:1-2; Hebrews 10:23-25; 13:1-5

humans need to learn how to cooperate with their partners in love and unity.[74]

As penguins must return to the sea to feed, we need both physical food and spiritual nourishment. The Bible affirms that "man does not live on bread alone, but on every word that comes from the mouth of God." Regular study of and meditation on divinely inspired writings is therefore necessary.[75]

The penguins provide from their own bodies specially adapted liquid food for their young, but they themselves dive deep to find the solid food they need. The Word of God likewise needs to be presented in a digestible form appropriate to the spiritual maturity of those receiving it. New disciples require spiritual milk, while those who are mature need to go into more depth and learn to dig out the "meat". Parts of Scripture are deep indeed, and without the enlightenment of the Holy Spirit, they remain an incomprehensible mystery.[76]

The Antarctic summer, during which penguins can enjoy sun, light, and an abundance of food, is only a short period of three to four months. Similarly, our lives are relatively brief and the time we have for serving God and humanity is short. The Bible reminds us that night will come when it will be no

---

[74] Ecclesiastes 4:9; Ephesians 5:22-33; 6:1-4
[75] Matthew 4:4
[76] 1 Corinthians 2:9-13, 3:2; 1 Peter 1:1-3; Hebrews 5:12-13

longer possible to work. Therefore it is important to make the most of existing opportunities.[77]

The penguin life cycle is characterized by help and deliverance arriving in the nick of time. At times, trials and difficulties in life stretch us to our limit. It has been remarked, however, that while God is seldom early, he is never late – it seems that often help comes in the last minute. If we learn to wait for God and not fear, we will be blessed. In his mercy, God does not test us beyond our endurance. While we may despair and almost lose hope, he will still be there, even if invisibly, helping and strengthening us. The biblical stories of Daniel and his friends are an example.[78]

As the only animals in Antarctica that stay to breed on the open ice and in winter, penguins are driven by an internal clock to assemble and start the trek inland for their winter mission. On occasion, God leads us – almost drives us – to do the seemingly impossible, but always provides a way. As Jesus Christ was brought by the Holy Spirit to the desert to be tempted, now and then we find ourselves in difficult situations to learn lessons or be purified. The Scriptures also describe circumstances where God led contrary to established wisdom or common sense, yet

---

[77] John 9:4
[78] 1 Corinthians 10:13; 2 Corinthians 1:8; Hebrews 13:5; Daniel 3:12-29; 6:1-24

every time he intervened miraculously and was glorified in the eyes of the beholders.[79]

None of us cherishes hardship and trials. Yet, paradoxically, challenging situations have a way of bringing out some of the finest qualities in us, as well as strengthening and purifying our character. Interestingly, the church has thrived in times of adversity, whereas in times of prosperity it hasn't done so well. And so, when hard times come, God may be working in our lives powerfully.[80]

In conclusion, even though penguins don't cross our paths very often, they can teach us lessons such as the importance of community, cooperation, bearing one another's burdens, making the most of opportunities, resourcefulness and ingenuity, and patient endurance. While penguins are internally programmed to do what they do, we need to consciously develop many of these qualities.

However, we aren't just left to our own limited resources. The God that programmed and equipped penguins to survive in the harsh Antarctic conditions provides for the needs of all creatures. We are specifically promised that God will supply our needs, come to our aid in times of need, and never forsake

---

[79] Matthew 4:1; 19:26; Mark 10:23-27; Luke 1:34-37; 18:27; Psalm 37:1-9, 34
[80] James 1:2-4; 1 Peter 1:6-9; 2:19-24; Romans 8:28; Revelation 2:8-10; 3:17-19

us. So whenever we find ourselves in challenging situations, we can trust that we'll receive the strength and wisdom to deal with them and come out stronger on the other side.[81]

---

[81] Luke 12:22-28; 2 Corinthians 9:8-12; Philippians 4:19; James 1:2-5; Hebrews 13:5; 1 Peter 1:6-7

The Amazing Date Palm

The palm trees stand straight and majestic in the park opposite our Saudi Arabian apartment – some taller than others and all with an impressive crown of large green fronds. The topmost fronds stretch toward heaven, reminiscent of praying arms. The lower ones reach sideways toward their neighbours or downwards. When dry, the bottom fronds are lopped off by gardeners for aesthetic and practical reasons – or, after a time, they fall off by themselves.

During the day, the palms provide shade and relief from the blazing sun and a perch for birds yelling at the occasional cat below. At night, under a full moon, they offer a romantic setting for lovers enjoying the cooler air. The sub-continental workers still use palm fronds as brooms to sweep the paths. Irrigation sprinklers under each palm automatically come on once or twice each day, ensuring that the trees are well watered.

History

The history of the palm goes back almost to the beginning of civilization in Mesopotamia, Egypt, and North East Africa. Oases and wadis with palms have enabled people to inhabit remote regions and cross vast deserts. In the desert areas of the Middle East, palms were valued not only for their easy-to-transport, high-energy, self-preserving fruit, but were also used for building construction. The trunk and fronds provided material for roofs, doors, and even utensils. Every part of the tree was utilized.

Today, the palm is found in warm areas around the world, including the desert regions of the United States and Australia. Its main benefits are the fruit, shade and decoration in the otherwise barren landscapes. The fruit is grown in cultivated plantations or in orchards where the offshoots are thinned to give the trees optimal conditions for fruit production.

Growth of Palm Trees

The palm needs a warm to hot climate and much water for flowering and fruit development. It is uniquely equipped to withstand extreme heat of 50 degrees Celsius or more, provided it is sufficiently irrigated. Only one growth point exists at the top from where both new fronds and flowers develop.

This enables tender young shoots to be insulated and protected by the old till they are strong enough to withstand the hot sun. Palms also have an internal cooling system whereby water from the soil travels through the roots up the trunk to the fronds and evaporates from the surface.

While requiring more than the average amount of water, the palm can thrive on all kinds of soil, including those which are sandy or have a high salt content. It can reach an age of over 100 years and grow up to 24 metres in height, but it is usually cut before then because in the latter years, the fruit yield declines and the tree becomes too tall for climbing safely. Being *dioecious*, it has separate male and female trees. A female tree needs to be pollinated by a male tree to bear fruit.

Fruit of the Palm

The fruit of the palm is a berry growing in clusters, which are often thinned during the 200-day growth cycle so that individual dates are bigger and of better quality. The palm fruit is unique in that it can be harvested at three of its five stages of development. Each stage has an Arabic name and distinct characteristics. Dates are rich in vitamins A and B, as well as in minerals, including potassium, calcium, iron, copper, magnesium, sulphur and phosphorus.

During the first stage, *hababauk*, 1-4 weeks after pollination, the female flower is small and creamy white. Through the next 5-17 weeks, during the *kimri* stage, the berry is green and slowly changes to yellow or red, depending on the date variety. It increases significantly in size, weight, and water content as it approaches its first stage of maturity.

At the *khalaal* stage, at 16-18 weeks, the fruit is considered commercially mature. It does not gain much weight and its water content decreases from 85% to 50-60%.

At the *rutab* stage, around 18-20 weeks, the fruit softens and its tips turn brown. Its water content further decreases and it is sold as fresh fruit.

The last stage, *tamr*, is marked by a water content of about 25%, a dark brown colour, as well as high glucose and fructose content. The fruit is now self-preserving. This is the exported type found in the supermarkets of countries where palms are not grown.

Palms in the Bible

The Scriptures refer to soils, trees, pruning, and fruit bearing in a number of places. The palm tree itself is mentioned in the Bible twenty-three times. Palm branches were used at festive occasions, such as during the Feast of Tabernacles or to welcome Christ as the Messiah King entering Jerusalem shortly before his crucifixion.[82]

The palm tree was an ever-present symbol in Solomon's temple, together with flowers and cherubim. It is also featured in Ezekiel's futuristic vision of the temple. In both cases, engraved palms cover walls and gates from top to bottom. Early Jewish synagogues were adorned with similar motifs. Trees, flowers and cherubim are reminiscent of the lost Paradise, which can symbolically be regained only through atonement in God's sanctuary.[83]

Spiritual Parallels

The Scriptures compare a virtuous person to a flourishing fruit-bearing tree planted by the waters – possibly a palm tree, given the predominance of palms in the Middle East. Water is analogous of the Holy Spirit, and just as the palm needs water to thrive, the just person needs a steady supply of the Holy Spirit to make wise choices and follow the right path in life.[84]

As the palm stretches its fronds both heavenward and sideways, the Spirit-led person reaches out, first upward toward God and secondly outward toward

---

[82] Leviticus 23:40; John 12:12-15
[83] 1 Kings 6:29-7:36; Ezekiel 40:16-41:26; Psalms 52:8; See also NIV Study Bible note on 1 Kings 6:29.
[84] Psalm 1:3; 92:12-14; John 4:10-14; Galatians 5:16, 25

neighbour, thereby fulfilling the two great love commandments. Not only does he or she cherish time in fellowship and communion with God, but also desires to reach out to others in practical, loving ways.[85]

Just as the palm is fruitful even in poor soil as long as it has enough water, we too, if watered from within by the Holy Spirit, can be productive no matter what the external circumstances. By remaining in Christ, the source of spiritual life, we will bear good fruit in our lives, thereby glorifying God.[86]

Periodically, palms need pruning. Gardeners remove dead, unproductive or weak parts of a tree for increased fruitfulness and better fruit quality. An unfruitful tree may be cut down altogether. Similarly, in our lives, God the Father does spiritual pruning or discipline – but always out of love and for our ultimate good. Through sometimes painful circumstances, destructive habits and practices are brought to our attention. They then need to be addressed and changed so that our fruitfulness can resume and continue to increase.[87]

As the palm endures the scorching heat of the desert, but is cooled by water evaporation from its leaves, for us the heat of painful trials or correction is

---

[85] Mark 12:29-33; 1 Thessalonians 5:17; Ephesians 6:18; 2 Thessalonians 1:11; James 2:14-17
[86] John 4:10-14; 7:38-39; 15:1-8; Romans 7:4
[87] John 15:1-2; Hebrews 12:5-13; Luke 13:6-9; Matthew 3:10

tempered and made bearable by God's faithful presence and the comfort of the Holy Spirit. We experience both hardship and God's comfort, so that we can then understand and come alongside others who suffer to comfort and encourage them.[88]

Reflecting on the amazing palm tree whose home is in the desert regions of the earth, we are reminded that we too are desert wanderers in the spiritual barrenness of this world. The hot sun of adversity may be beating on our heads, but the life-giving refreshment and comfort of the divine Spirit sustains us. May our lives be productive like the palm, bearing the fruit of love, peace and kindness, nourishing those who cross our paths, and glorifying our Father in heaven.[89]

---

[88] Deuteronomy 31:6-8; Psalm 118:6-7; Hebrews 13:5; 1 Corinthians 10:13; 2 Corinthians 1:3-6; John 14:16-18
[89] Galatians 5:22-25; 1 Peter 4:12-19

Pond Flowers

Large leaves, typical of water lilies, covered the pond surface. Yet the usual water lily flowers were few and far between. Instead, there were dozens of small, white, delicate flowers, each about two centimetres in diameter, with fringed petals and a yellow centre. Fascinated by their design and beauty and wanting to take a closer look, I knelt down to pick one of the flowers near the shore. I was surprised that what I thought to be a single flower came up with a whole cluster of stalked buds attached to a large leaf. I took it home and placed it in a large bowl of water near the kitchen window.

Later I learned that this interesting plant was a water snowflake (*Nymphoides indica*), a relative of the water lily family. It grows in still, shallow water and is attached to the bottom by root tubers or rhizomes. A leaf with flowers that is not attached will grow roots to attach itself and take nutrients from the soil.

For about ten days in our kitchen, the flowers opened, sometimes one a day, sometimes two or three. Overnight, the stalks grew taller and in the morning, there were one or more buds above the water surface. By around ten o'clock, the flower was open in all its glory. It remained strikingly beautiful till mid-afternoon, but around four o'clock it started closing, and by sunset it was finished. The stalk bent over and became submerged again.

The next morning, another bud or two opened, bloomed for six to eight hours, then closed and died. The leaf that sustained the flowers gradually deteriorated, and in a little over a week it also died – probably because it couldn't root itself in the bowl. The experience brought to mind how the Bible uses flowers as a symbol for the shortness of life.[90] One can indeed draw some interesting parallels.

Flowers as a Life Metaphor

Human life can be seen starting like a bud. While cute in appearance, a child does not have the physical beauty of an adolescent or young adult. Like an opening bud, the youngster grows in size and matures physically. By the end of puberty, it is fully developed. A sixteen to twenty-five year old woman is physically more attractive than she will be at any other time in

---

[90] Job 14:1-2; Psalm 103:15; Isaiah 40:6-8; James 1:9-11

her life. She is not unlike a beautiful flower in full bloom – smooth complexion, shiny hair, slender body, sharpness of mind and senses – an exquisite picture of youth.

A decade or two later, however, the physical beauty has gradually waned, and this continues to old age and eventual death. With increasing age, there are more wrinkles, more body fat, greying hair, as well as deteriorating eyesight and hearing – all signs of wear and tear with the passage of time. In their existential *angst*, some get discouraged at the thought of their physical state and destiny. Fortunately, however, this is not the end of the story – the Bible holds out an encouraging hope.

While the body ages and degenerates, those indwelt by the Holy Spirit are experiencing an internal renewal. As the outward person loses their beauty and slowly perishes, the inner one is becoming more attractive through the working of the Spirit. Growth in wisdom and virtue surpasses the importance of physical beauty.

However, as the water snowflake leaf needs to be attached to the rhizome in the soil at the bottom of the pond, the child of God needs to be rooted in Jesus Christ. Unless we abide in and remain in our Saviour, we have no future beyond this declining physical existence.[91]

The glory we admire in this life – be it that of a water snowflake or a stunningly beautiful woman in her prime – will grow totally dim in comparison to our future glory. The Scriptures reveal that through a resurrection from the dead, corruption will be transformed into incorruption, weakness into power, natural body into spiritual body, temporary existence into eternal life. We will see the risen Christ in his glory, and even more amazingly, we will be like him![92]

How incredible is the love of God, who created glorious things on the earth, but left far greater glories beyond this life for the age to come. If the created world awes us now, how much more do we have to look forward to in the new heaven and new earth![93]

---

[91] Proverbs 31:30; John 15:5-6; 2 Corinthians 3:18; 4:16-18; Colossians 3:9-10; Ephesians 3:16-19; 4:22-24; 1 Peter 1:22-25
[92] Romans 8:11; 1 Corinthians 15:42-44; Colossians 1:27; 1 John 3:2; Revelation 1:10-16
[93] Revelation 21:1-7; 22:1-5

Growing Cherry Tomatoes

Admiring a neighbour's garden patch on a late spring morning in Brisbane, I shared how I had recently planted some cherry tomato seeds, but met with no success. In response, she picked one of her own tomatoes, saying "Here. Try planting this one."

I planted the seeds – half of them directly in the soil and the others in a small flower pot which I left outside. About a week later, tiny green shoots appeared on top of the soil. Then two leaves, followed by more leaves, and the seedlings slowly began to look like small tomato plants.

For several mornings I found the pot and its tiny seedlings disturbed by a bird or some other creature during the night. I therefore decided to take the pot inside and place it on the kitchen counter near the window. As they grew, the seedlings kept turning toward the light, even when I turned them back. The seedlings outside all germinated together in one spot and grew straight up. At first they grew a little slower than those in the pot as they each had less room.

After another couple of weeks, the time came for replanting to give each of the seedlings more space. I placed them all into larger containers with good soil. With warm, sunny days and daily watering, the plants grew rapidly – though the group from the kitchen, initially a little taller, for some reason began to lag behind. First I thought they had too much sun, so I moved them, but to no avail. Only when I added some blood and bone fertilizer to the purchased soil did they green up and begin to grow.

Each seedling first continued to grow new leaves, then they started branching out, and then came the exciting day, about six weeks after germination, when the first cluster of buds appeared. Insects began to hover around the small yellow flowers and before long, after about a week to ten days, the flowers turned into tiny green fruit – no more than a millimetre in diameter.

New flower clusters have developed since the first fruit appeared. That first fruit, now about two weeks old, has grown to about twenty millimetres in diameter – in that short time, it has increased about twentyfold. And the other flower clusters, now around twenty-five in number, are also slowly turning into clusters of ripening fruit – each containing 4-6 cherry tomatoes. I can't wait for the first tomato to turn red and be ready to harvest. While I'm waiting, I thought I'd share the following reflections.

Lessons for Life

I'll begin with a closer look at the seeds. My single cherry tomato has given rise to ten plants – each with the potential of perhaps fifty cherry tomatoes. A thousandfold gain or 5000% increase! This in addition to the fact that the seeds of those tomatoes could be planted again for another tomato crop!

In nature, every seed, be it a weed, flower, vegetable or a tree, has incredible potential within. In one tiny seed lies the making of the whole plant with its stems, leaves, flowers and fruit. Many plants are perennial and may yield a harvest for years – amounting to thousands of pieces of fruit or vegetables – each with seeds and the potential to give rise to more crop-producing plants of the same kind. What a staggering increase from just a single seed!

We humans, too, are like seeds with an amazing potential within us – specifically a divine potential. Created in God's image, we are already in a sense divine offspring and are one day destined to fully take on the glorified image of Jesus Christ, the divine Son of God.[94]

---

[94] Acts 17:28-29; Romans 8:29; Colossians 3:4; 1 John 3:1-2

Since we are destined for divine glory, our responsibility here and now is to develop our potential for this and our ultimate life. We need to discover and develop our gifts and talents and then use them for the benefit of others – not only fellow humans, but all living beings. According to the Scriptures, humans were given charge over the other creatures, but have unfortunately greatly abused this God-given responsibility. All life really is special and sacred and needs to be regarded and treated as such, rather than being exploited and abused out of greed and for selfish gain. Those who are destroying the earth will ultimately suffer consequences.[95]

The original seed bears the programming for the timing of all the phases of the plant life cycle, such as when to start creating buds for leaves and flowers and when the flowers should turn into ripening fruit. Strong evidence of innate intelligence lies behind the life cycle and development of any plant. Why, for example, do some plants first grow leaves and then develop flowers, and other plants do it the other way around? Our minds and bodies, too, have inbuilt timing for their development. By analogy, in childhood we sprout and develop leaves, in youth and early adulthood we bloom, in our thirties and there-

---

[95] Genesis 1:26-31; Revelation 11:18

after we bear fruit, and in our senior years, we start to contract and shed leaves.

While certain aspects of our lives are internally programmed or influenced by external circumstances, we also have a part to play in the fruit and results of our lives. These largely depend on the seeds we have sown. The Scriptures broadly refer to two types of seeds, yielding two basic life directions and outcomes. One is to sow to the Spirit and reap the fruit of the Spirit – such as love, peace, kindness and gentleness, leading ultimately to eternal life. The other is to sow to the ego and produce the "works of the flesh" – including hate, quarrels, jealousy and murder, leading in the end to reaping eternal death.[96]

In our lives, a universal law of cause and effect also operates, meaning that we reap what we have sown. The "harvest" – be it from sowing good seeds like tomato plants, or bad seeds like weeds – is usually, as in nature, not immediate, but does come, and we'll receive more than we have sown.[97] Sometimes the results of our good actions don't come when we expect or hope for them, but again, with patience, we'll find they do arrive – even if perhaps not in the way we anticipate. For example, some writers, performers, or other artists work hard for years before they

---

[96] Matthew 25:46; Romans 6:22-23; Galatians 5: 16-26
[97] Job 4:8; Proverbs 11:18; 22:8; Hosea 8:7; 2 Corinthians 9:6; Galatians 6:7-8

have a breakthrough. In our time, this has been the case of the now famous Andre Rieu and his orchestra. The greatness of some men and women was only recognized after their death. Patience and perseverance, together with underlying hope, are needed in waiting for our garden fruit and vegetables to ripen, as well as for the rewards of our life's activities to become manifest.

Non-virtuous actions and allowing bad habits or deeds to continue may also not bring about immediate consequences. In fact this is why crime as well as unhealthy lifestyles continue and increase. A chain smoker, for example, despite countless warnings, thinks that nothing will happen to them if they keep on smoking. Then, 40 or 50 years later, they are diagnosed with cancer. Life in many ways is a mystery and some situations are difficult to understand. War criminals, for instance, may not get justly punished before their death – on the contrary, they may live out their lives in ease and comfort, despite having caused others untold suffering. But perhaps there is more to the story and we haven't seen the end yet.[98]

To grow, bloom and bear fruit, plants need water, sun and soil containing the essential nutrients. We, too, need spiritual nourishment (as well as physical)

---

[98] Psalm 37:7-40; Jeremiah 12:1-17

to grow, develop and bear fruit. The Bible teaches us that "Man does not live on bread alone, but on every word that comes out of the mouth of God." In addition to "the bread of life", we also need the living water of the Holy Spirit and the light of Christ – "the Sun of righteousness".[99]

My tomato seeds sprouted and grew roots some time before they became visible above the soil. Often in our lives, changes are occurring within our hearts and minds before we become aware of them. The Holy Spirit works behind the scenes and the effects are not immediately apparent. Often it is only retrospectively that we notice changes in our thinking and reactions, or perhaps those close to us may make an encouraging comment – the seeds planted in our hearts have then come into view.

The tomato plants in my grow-box and pots grew stalks and leaves, but ultimately the fruit bearing is what counts – a tomato plant with just a lot of leafage is of little interest and value. Likewise, God desires for us to bear fruit. The Scriptures give several metaphors and parables on this theme. Our fruit is how we act and behave towards others – our outward actions. This shows what kind of people we are – what is inside, in our hearts, manifests on the outside. Are we motivated by the Holy Spirit and therefore loving,

---

[99] Matthew 4:4; Malachi 4:2; Luke 1:76-79; John 6:35, 48; 7:37-39; Ephesians 5:14

peaceful, generous and compassionate? Or, are we following the dark side of our ego and acting in unkind, miserly, dishonest and angry ways toward fellow humans and other creatures? It is our good fruit, brought about through our abiding with Jesus Christ and the Spirit, that glorifies God in our lives.[100]

Fruit takes time to grow and ripen – sometimes it is the slowest part of the seasonal growth cycle. Also, some plants produce fruit faster than other plants or trees. For example, in the spring, strawberries, cherries and apple trees may blossom roughly at the same time, but strawberries and cherries ripen much faster than the apples. This may be analogous to the differences among people – some mature spiritually faster than others. Observing how sometimes fruit takes a long time to develop, we can only be patient with ourselves and others. In due time, if we continue in well-doing, we shall reap. And we are promised a glorious harvest in the divine kingdom.[101]

---

[100] Matthew 7:16-20; Luke 6:43; 13:6-9; John 15:2-8; Romans 7:4-6; Colossians 1:10
[101] Romans 22-25; 12:12; 1 Corinthians 13:4; Galatians 5:22; Ephesians 4:2; Colossians 3:12; James 5:7-8

About the Author

Eva Peck has a Christian and international backround. Through Christian work as well as teaching English as a second language in several countries, she has experienced a range of cultures, customs and environments. Having lived and worked in Australia, the United States, Europe, Asia, and the Middle East, she now draws on those experiences in her writing.

Eva refers to biblical passages in this book the way she has come to understand them. Having had the opportunity to fellowship with Christians from a variety of faith traditions, she also recognizes that many faith-related issues can be understood in more than one way.

Eva studied biological sciences as well as theology at the tertiary level and has a Bachelors degree in science and Masters degree in Theology. She lives in Brisbane, Australia, with her husband, Alexander. The Pecks' other books of spiritual nature include *Pathway to Life – through the Holy Scriptures* and

Journey to the Divine Within – through Silence, Stillness and Simplicity. Both publications, as well as their other books can be ordered online through www.pathway-publishing.org.

More About the Author's Other Books

Divine Reflections in Times and Seasons

This book looks at times and seasons and explores how everyday phenomena mirror spiritual realities. Readers are encouraged to take a fresh look at a sunrise, the sunlight on trees and flowers, the creatures that cross their path, and the starry heavens, among other things, and contemplate the meaning of it all.

Divine Reflections in Natural Phenomena

This volume explores how spiritual realities can be glimpsed in the world of nature – in phenomena such as life and its order, the beauty and harmony around us, and the countless mysteries of the heaven and the earth.

Divine Insights from Human Experience

This is a collection of writings drawn from the author's experience. Each piece begins with a story and is followed by reflections on the wisdom and/or spiritual insights gleaned from the various incidents. The book consists of two parts – *Wisdom from Life* and *Spiritual Analogies from Life*.

Pathway to Life – Through the Holy Scriptures

Pathway to Life presents in a concise and systematic way the basic teachings of the Bible. It strives to offer a balanced, non-denominational understanding of the Scriptures. Conclusions are supported by scripture references.

Journey to the Divine Within – Through Silence, Stillness and Simplicity

Journey to the Divine Within shares, through the reflections of a variety of spiritual writers, how to enter the realm of one's heart. One way that this occurs is through silence, stillness and simplicity. When pondered, the reflections will lead readers to the silence and stillness of their own hearts on the path to encountering the Life, Light and Love within.

Other Resources

Eva Peck has created several websites with spiritual content. Feel free to browse and explore.

Truth & Beauty
(www.truth-and-beauty.org)

This site seeks to capture what is true and lovely. With the aim of helping readers appreciate the nature of reality, it deals with practical and spiritual aspects of life. To uplift and edify, it provides galleries with beautiful nature images as well as heartwarming stories.

Pathway to Life
(www.pathway-to-life.org)

The site presents the essential Christian message under 36 biblical topics in Q & A style. Where several denominational views exist regarding a subject, these are covered as different interpretations. Supporting scriptures are given throughout. The information is also available in book form.

Heaven's Reflections
(www.heavens-reflections.org)

The site features the theme of seeing the extraordinary in the ordinary, the sacred in the daily, and the special in the routine. It focuses on how the world around us, upon deeper looking, reflects spiritual realities. This book, *Divine Reflections in Living Things*, is based on the content of the website as are its two companion volumes *Divine Reflections in Natural Phenomena* and *Divine Reflections in Living Things*.

You may also enjoy visiting Alexander's websites:

Spirituality for Life
(www.spirituality-for-life.org)

The site shares information with the aim of presenting a practical spirituality to enhance one's life journey and to help fulfil one's divine destiny.

Prayer of the Heart – Journey to the Divine Within
(www.prayer-of-the-heart.org)

This site deals with the prayer of the heart, or meditation, covered from a mainly Christian perspective. It features quotations from a variety of spiritual writers. The content is also available in book form.

See also **www.pathway-publishing.org** for the Pecks' other creations.

Readers' Comments

Thank you kindly for your book series Divine Reflections. I have skimmed through the previews and think that the books are indeed wonderful. I think that your work and words will be an inspiration to the many people that need them in this difficult world in which we are living. You have the experience, knowledge, ability and the spiritual background to reach out to people to give them hope. Well done!
Pauline G., Cairo, Egypt

Your style of writing is very readable and sympathetic, and the way you reflect on the beauties of nature is lovely. Your message and discussion is soft and gentle and makes the reader feel God's love.
Margaret S., Thornlands, Australia

I found your book to be a blend of the cosmic Christ you have discovered in nature and the deep-rooted "word" which is imprinted in your heart.
Sadie M., Thornlands, Australia

The reflections on God's creation were delightful – it is so true, as the Bible tells us in Romans, that we can see the proof of the Creator in His handiwork all around us.
Jan H., Mittagong, Australia

I really liked these reflections and feel like universal truths come through and the words spoken are honest. I especially like the part about "lessons from desert cats". It is so sweet and delicate to think about animals in that way.
Lobat A., Ryiadh, Saudi Arabia

It is amazing how God works. It is easy to see pigeons fighting, but very difficult to understand the messages they are sending. Thank God that He gives people wisdom to understand and share with others.
Francis F., Ryiadh, Saudi Arabia

About Pathway Publishing

Pathway Publishing is dedicated to sharing truth and beauty by publishing books that present what is true to life and reality, as well as what is lovely and inspirational. The goal is to not only provide sound information, but also to lift the human spirit.

Pathway Publishing has a vision of helping readers on their path of enlightenment and spiritual transformation. The wisdom and experience of spiritual teachers, thinkers, and visionary writers from various backgrounds and faith traditions are recognized and valued.

Other books produced by Pathway Publishing, beside the *Divine Reflections* trilogy, are:
- *Divine Insights from Human Life*, Eva Peck
- *Pathway to Life - Through the Holy Scriptures*, Eva and Alexander Peck
- *Journey to the Divine Within – Through Silence, Stillness and Simplicity*, Alexander and Eva Peck
- *Artistic Inspirations - Paintings of Jindrich Degen* arranged by Eva and Alexander Peck
- *Floral and Nature Art – Photography of Jindrich Degen* arranged by Eva and Alexander Peck
- *Memories of Times with Dad – Poems and Letters*, Alexander and Eva Peck
- *Volné verše,* Jindrich Degen (in Czech)
- *Verše pro dnešní dobu,* Jindrich Degen (in Czech)

Pathway Publishing
Seeking truth and beauty

www.ingramcontent.com/pod-product-compliance
Lightning Source LLC
Chambersburg PA
CBHW031256290426
44109CB00012B/600